Favorite Words
OF
Famous People

Also by Lewis Burke Frumkes

Wall Street Laid Bear

How to Raise Your IQ by Eating Gifted Children

*Mensa Think Smart Book: Games & Puzzles to Develop a
Sharper, Quicker Mind* (co-author)

Name Crazy: What Your Name Really Means

Manhattan Cocktail

Metapunctuation

The Logophile's Orgy

Favorite Words OF Famous People

A Celebration of Superior Words from Writers, Educators, Scientists, and Humorists

LEWIS BURKE FRUMKES

Marion Street Press
Portland, Oregon

Published by Marion Street Press
4207 SE Woodstock Blvd # 168
Portland, OR 97206-6267
USA
http://www.marionstreetpress.com/
Orders and review copies: 800-888-4741

Printed in the United States of America
ISBN 978-1-933338-90-3

Cover art direction by Nicky Ip

Back cover photo credits:

Lawrence Block photo by Philippe Auray
Mary Higgins Clark photo by Bernard Vidal
Steven Pinker photo by Rebecca Goldstein
Gish Jen photo by Michael Lionstar
Susan Isaacs photo by Sigrid Estrada
Howard Gardner photo by Jay Gardner
Joseph Finder photo by Joel Benjamin
Walter Mosley photo by David Burnett

Library of Congress Cataloging-in-Publication Data

Frumkes, Lewis Burke.
  Favorite words of famous people / Lewis Burke Frumkes.
      p. cm.
  ISBN 978-1-933338-90-3 (pbk.)
  1. Lexicology—Anecdotes. 2. Vocabulary—Anecdotes. I. Title.
  PE1574.F723 2011
  428.1—dc23
                                              2011018642

For Alana, Timothy, Amber, Scott, Carola and Becket ...
six words that I love.

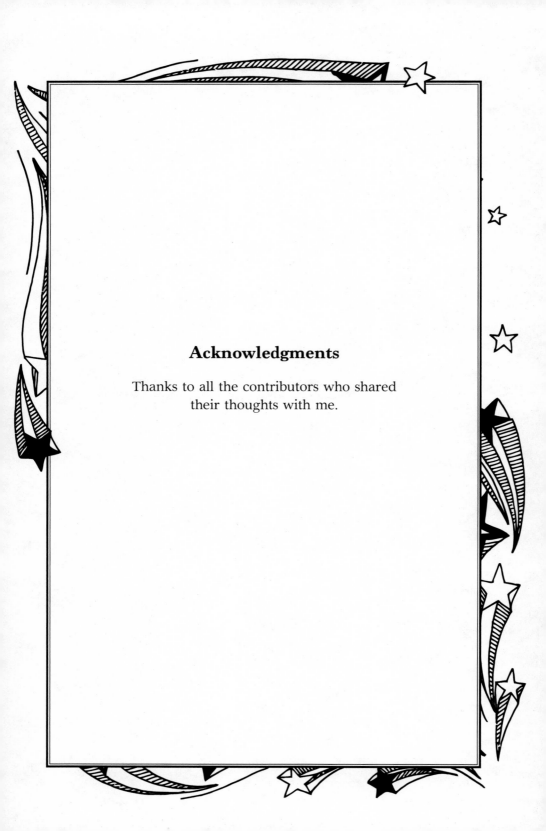

Acknowledgments

Thanks to all the contributors who shared
their thoughts with me.

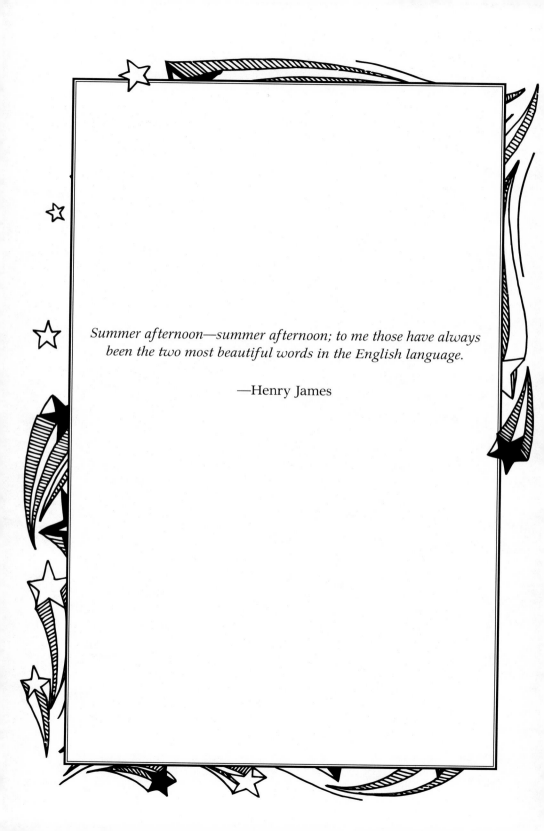

Summer afternoon—summer afternoon; to me those have always been the two most beautiful words in the English language.

—Henry James

Author's Introduction

Collecting words from people is almost as much fun as the words themselves.

After I shook hands with Hillary Clinton at a dinner some years ago for the United Cerebral Palsy Foundation where she was receiving an award, I asked her for her favorite word. With a smile she gave me "love." When I asked Jules Feiffer who was sitting in my office for his word, he asked me for a piece of my stationary and there right in front of me drew an illustration for his "word of wisdom," as he called it, "DUCK." The illustration never published before is included in this book. When I met Muhammad Ali at a dinner for the American Ireland Fund in 2011, his lovely wife, Lonnie Ali, standing by his side gave me his favorite words "The Greatest" and I felt humbled to finally meet "The Greatest" in person. Each word collected has a story of its own and Richard Johnson even gave me a second word, which I have added to the saucy word he gave me years ago.

Favorite Words began as a wondering about other writers' favorite words, then grew into a project far beyond anything I had originally envisioned. Contributors one and all were un-abashedly enthusiastic about complying with my query and often confessed to never having considered the question before. Through the responses sometimes one could discern the very landscape of a contributor's mind, or his vision of life. When not being profound or revealing, contributors were frequently witty or linguistically clever. Others were just direct and succinct.

The thrust of the book is that we all have favorite words, words that tickle our ears and please our eyes, words that we seem to use more often than other words. I, for example, use the words "eggplant" and "kumquat" more often in my writing than other words, though this may have more to do with the shape of the objects, ovoid, than with the sounds of the words ... I'm an egg man. Actually, if you noticed, I've used the word "more," Wilbur Ross's favorite word, more than "eggplant" or "kumquat" here, in fact more than I'd like in this one paragraph. Six times to be exact. If you pushed me further, I'd tell you that "djinn" and "fey" and perhaps "seductive," "oneiric," and "enchantment" are favorite words as well because they are magical and mysterious, not to mention romantic.

Judith Kelman wrote that "serendipity" was her favorite word, and Helen Handley too, and from Sri Lanka came Arthur C. Clarke's explanation of the origin of "serendipity"; it comes from his adopted country, Serendib, or Serendip, the ancient term for Ceylon. Like Leibnitz and Newton, who independently invented the calculus, Margaret Atwood and Fred Mustard Stewart both alighted on one of English's most obscure of words among their favorites, "chthonic," which means of or pertaining to the gods of the underworld.

Writers, for the most part, are more sensitive to words than other people, because they use them all the time, and work with them, and sometimes bend them to their will. In fact, that is what got me doing this book in the first place—I had favorite words and I was curious what other writers' favorite words might be. Nor did it come as a surprise when several of the writers queried declared "onomatopoeia," a writer's word, to be their favorite word, or that Wes Craven, Wilfrid Sheed, and Sven Birkerts chose "plangent," the incessant and repeating sound of waves rolling up on the beach. These are wonderful words, and writers are understandably attracted to them. Desmond Tutu, Anglican Bishop of Cape Town and a Nobel laureate for peace, as I recall, was enthralled by the word "wonderful" itself. Another group of contributors including columnist Ann Landers, publisher

Al Goldstein, and cookbook writer Maida Heatter confessed to an outsized fondness for "chocolate" as a word and as a substance. "Callipygian," a word I first discovered as a youngster while reading an obscure Spanish writer in Spanish, surfaced as the favorite word of two contributors, Patrick McGrath and Tommy Boyle, aka T. Coraghessan Boyle, who subsequently opted instead for "steatopygia."

Often writers literally love words, the way other people love children. They become almost possessive about them, which may account for why a few well-known writers insisted that they had no favorite words or at least were not willing to share them. Evan Hunter, a good friend who sadly later succumbed to throat cancer, for example said, "I've pondered and repondered your question, and for the life of me I cannot think of a favorite word. My favorite color is blue. Does that help?"

Nevertheless, I thought it would be useful and fun to see what many good writers, as well as scientists, educators, actors, and others who work with language, would find to be their favorite words. And the results were not only gratifying but on occasion actually astounding. In fact, as I mentioned earlier, what started as just a whimsical anthological work became an adventure so fascinating I couldn't wait to open the mail each day to see what the catch would bring. People poured their cleverness, their aesthetics, and often their hearts into their contributions, and you will enjoy these in just a moment.

Ray Bradbury selected "cinnamon," because it "causes me to think of voyages and ships on the sea and the *Arabian Nights*." John Updike responded with "anfractuous" and "phosphorescent" because that is how the world appeared to him when he was sixty. I wonder if any of us were John Updike, wouldn't we also see the world as aglow and phosphorescent? But Russell Baker, the great *New York Times* columnist known for his wit, curiously chose "melancholy" as one of his favorite words, and then added, "But if proper nouns may be considered, no word satisfies me more utterly than 'Pushtunistan.'" Larry King predictably and charmingly chose "why" as his word. Not only is

it a word he uses professionally he says, but "it is the best word in the universe. Think about it."

Does genetics play a role in favorite words? Susan and Ben Cheever, sister and brother writers, independently and at different times sent me the words "yes" and "no" with contrasting reasons for their selections. John Kluge and Oscar de la Renta, who are not related, affirmed their fondness for the positive word "yes." However, Bel Kaufman, who recently celebrated her 100th birthday, preferred "no," and then added that she didn't learn to deploy it successfully until she was sixty-five.

Abundantly forthcoming, as you would expect, were master wordsmiths Richard Lederer and Willard Espy, whose love of words was clearly reflected in their colorful selections of "usher" and "velleity." One linguistics mandarin (Noam Chomsky), on the other hand, when approached for a favorite word, said he'd think about it but that he wasn't really good at this sort of thing, which caused one wag to suggest I write back "if not you, then who?"

Joyce Carol Oates showed a definite fondness for "palimpsest"; Erica Jong, for "breath," reminding us that there is only one other word in the English language rhyming with "breath," and that is "death"; and Dave Barry, for "weasel." Leo Buscaglia, Ricardo Montalban, and Rosanno Brazzi, like Hillary, were in love with "love," though each in his or her own special way. It got so that each day was an adventure in finding more fabulous words from other interesting and exciting people. Nobel laureates in physics Arno Penzias, Sheldon Glashow, and Frank Wilczeck sent in their favorite words, Penzias providing a moving glimpse of his life under Hitler in 1938 in Germany, and Glashow demonstrating his impressive knowledge of languages by choosing words with interesting double and triple letters, "radii" and "skiing" and "hajji" in English and *Schneeeule* in German, and then pointing out that "indivisibility" has more *i*'s than any other English word he knows except its plural, which has seven. Henry Rosovsky, former dean of the School of Arts and Sciences at Harvard and the principal architect of the core curriculum, sent in the best definition of a liberal education that he had ever come across as his contribution to favorite words, and Willard V. O. Quine, one of this century's preeminent philosopher/logicians, wrote that Donald Davidson, another great philosopher, had told him he overdoes the word "actually," though he (Quine) is unaware of having any particular fondness for it.

Animals had their day. Margaret Drabble did a turn on "squirrels" and Pamela McCorduck on "frogs." And then more fabulous words arrived from Quentin Crisp and Cynthia Ozick; from Helen Gurley Brown, Dominick Dunne, Ed McMahon, Douglas Fairbanks, Jr., Gene Kelly, and Gahan Wilson until my head began to swim from the delight of it all.

Patricia Volk, the author of *All It Takes*, said she was partial to *fuh-drayt*, *fuh-shimmeled*, *fuh-cocktub*, *fuh-blondget*, and *fuh-tushed*, five Yiddish words that mean crazy, mixed up, addled, lost, and wiped out. Just saying them, she says, and shrugging, makes you feel better. She also liked "euglena," as in the green protozoan with a single flagellum and a red pigment spot, and thereafter, to Pattie's amusement, I began to call her Euglena. "Euglena Volk," it has a certain ring, don't you think?

When it comes to choosing favorite words, there are many different approaches, but euphony is an apparently important and popular consideration. Language experts such as I. M. Pei, after examining some lists of most beautiful words from American and British writers in the forties, which included "dawn," "golden," "murmuring," and "lullaby," found that it was difficult to separate the words from their associations, and that perhaps the only objective way to measure the euphony of words would be to use judges who did not know the meanings of the words. In this regard, whether it originated with H. L. Mencken, who my friend Richard Lederer tells me once quoted a Chinese boy who was learning English as saying that "cellar door" contained the most musical combination of sounds he had ever heard in that language, or that it was just the result of one of those lists that keep turning up, in this case, "The Most Beautiful Words in the English Language," which had as a winner—"cellar door," it is perhaps coincidental that four of the contributors to *Favorite Words of Famous People* agreed by choosing "cellar door" as their favorite words as well.

Bruce Feirstein, who wrote *Real Men Don't Eat Quiche*, and who also loves the sounds of words, did not choose "quiche" but "flotilla" as his favorite word both for its special aural appeal and the appealing image it conjures up in his mind. Edgar Allan Poe more than many other poets understood how to make the sounds of words work for him and frequently employed "ore-sound" words such as "nevermore" and "lore" and "moor" to adumbrate (one of Ricardo Montalban's favorite words) the landscape of his poetry and convey a foreboding sense of gloom and forlornness. In case you hadn't noticed, persons writing love songs tend to employ *oo* words like "moon" and "croon" to create their special effects. "Moon over Miami, da, da, da, da, da, da ..." And soon everybody is making goo-goo eyes and cooing and wooing.

Fashion also counts, and fashionable words such as "cobble" and "jerry-built" and "tad" tend to become favorite words among those in the know and intellectuals, while words such as "sufficient," "proleptic," "necessary," and "apodictic" find currency with philosophers and psychologists. Close your eyes now ... okay, "shit," "fuck," and "schmuck" are also favorite words ... and "you know" unquestionably led the pack as chief locutional weed of the insecure and the inarticulate ... you know. Surprisingly and amusingly, two arch contributors to this book even wrote that "Frumkes" was their favorite word, if names could be counted as words. And I accept that. What could be more flattering?

In short, this word project became a real labor of "love"—Hillary Clinton's, Rosanno Brazzi's, and Leo Buscaglia's favorite word (see page *ix*)—and I genuinely enjoyed the year and a half it took me to complete it. I came to understand what Phyllis Diller meant when she wrote that words "are the playthings of the mind." Phyllis, now in her nineties, besides being a gifted

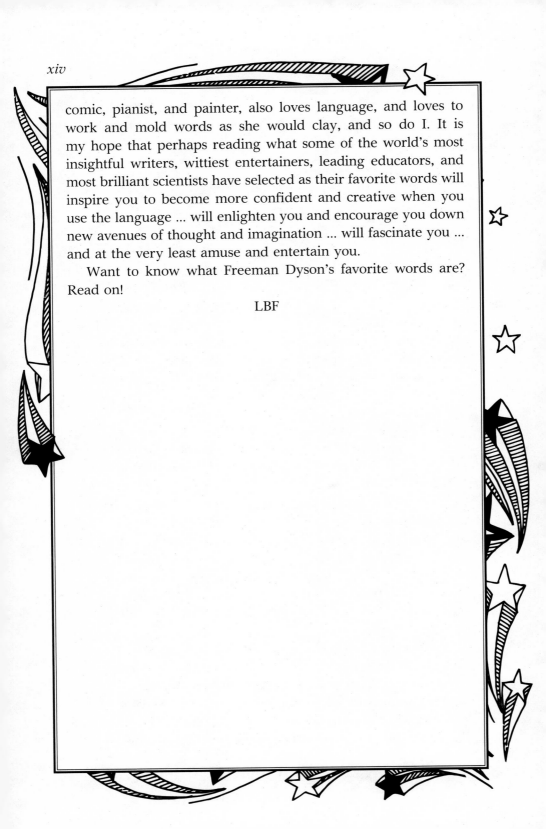

comic, pianist, and painter, also loves language, and loves to work and mold words as she would clay, and so do I. It is my hope that perhaps reading what some of the world's most insightful writers, wittiest entertainers, leading educators, and most brilliant scientists have selected as their favorite words will inspire you to become more confident and creative when you use the language ... will enlighten you and encourage you down new avenues of thought and imagination ... will fascinate you ... and at the very least amuse and entertain you.

Want to know what Freeman Dyson's favorite words are? Read on!

LBF

Contributors

Floyd Abrams
Diane Ackerman
Rob Ackerman
Hanan Al-Shaykh
Muhammad Ali
Norman Arnoff
John Ashbery
Margaret Atwood
Nicholson Baker
Russell Baker
David Baldacci
John Barth
Dave Barry
Kenneth Battelle
Julie Baumgold
William Baumol
Orson Bean
Ira Berkow
Anne Bernays
Sven Birkerts
Bruce Bliven
Naomi Bliven
Lawrence Block
Roy Blount, Jr.
Tom Bodett
T. Coraghessan Boyle
Ray Bradbury
Barbara Taylor Bradford
Rosanno Brazzi
Joe Bob Briggs
Helen Gurley Brown
Mario Buatta
Edna Buchanan
Leo Buscaglia

A. S. Byatt
Jeanne Cavelos
Ben Cheever
Susan Cheever
Ron Chernow
Mary Higgins Clark
Arthur C. Clarke
James Clavell
Hillary Rodham Clinton
Michael Connelly
Denton A. Cooley
Wes Craven
Quentin Crisp
Norm Crosby
Mario Cuomo
Clive Cussler
Scott Daspin
Olivia de Havilland
Len Deighton
Oscar de la Renta
Alan Dershowitz
Phyllis Diller
Rita Dove
Roddy Doyle
Dame Margaret Drabble
Dominick Dunne
Andrea Dworkin
Freeman Dyson
Fernanda Eberstadt
Paul Edwards
Albert Ellis
Alison Espach
Willard Espy
Gloria Estefan

Dame Edna Everage
Douglas Fairbanks, Jr.
Jules Feiffer
Bruce Feirstein
Joseph Finder
Gary Fisketjon
Milos Forman
Dick Francis
Richard Frances
Bruce Jay Friedman
Lewis Burke Frumkes
Melvin B. Frumkes
Roy Frumkes
Cristina Garcia
Howard Gardner
William H. Gass
Murray Gell-Mann
Paolo Giordano
Penn Gillette
Nikki Giovanni
Sheldon Glashow
Julia Glass
Harrison J. Goldin
AI Goldstein
Rebecca Goldstein
Adam Gopnik
Al Gore
Edward Gorey
Virginia Graham
Alan "Ace" Greenberg
Dan Greenburg
A. R. Gurney
Mark Hamill
Helen Handley
Donna Hanover
Josephine Hart

Don Hauptman
Maida Heatter
Florence Henderson
Tony Hendra
Bob Hope
A. E. Hotchner
Arianna Huffington
Derek Humphry
Evan Hunter
Susan Isaacs
Pico Iyer
Rona Jaffe
Dennis James
Morton Janklow
Tama Janowitz
Gish Jen
Franklyn G. Jenifer
Richard Jenrette
Richard Johnson
Erica Jong
Michio Kaku
Bel Kaufman
Gene Kelly
Judith Kelman
Rose Kennedy
Florence King
Larry King
John Kluge
Elizabeth Kostova
Paul Krassner
Charles Krauthammer
Bernard Kripke
Amy Kugali
Hedy Lamarr
Wally Lamb
Ann Landers

George Lang
Lewis Lapham
Ring Lardner, Jr.
Robin Leach
David Leavitt
Richard Lederer
Richard LeFrak
Elmore Leonard
Yiyun Li
Art Linkletter
Gordon Lish
Phillip Lopate
Shirley Lord
Iris Love
Robert Ludlum
Roa Lynn
Yo-Yo Ma
Sirio Maccioni
Jamie Malanowski
Yann Martel
Peter Mayle
Patrick McCabe
Colum McCann
Pamela McCorduck
Patrick McGrath
Ed McMahon
Larry McMurtry
Norman Mailer
Elaine Marks
Peter Martins
Bobbie Ann Mason
Daphne Merkin
Dina Merrill
Ricardo Montalban
Lorrie Moore
David Morrell

Desmond Morris
Frederic Morton
Georgette Mosbacher
Walter Mosley
Jerome T. Murphy
Susan Nagel
Audrey Niffenegger
Sigrid Nunez
Joyce Carol Oates
Sidney Offit
Ben Okri
Frank Oz
Cynthia Ozick
Abraham Pais
Orhan Pamuk
Richard Panek
Linus Pauling
Arno Penzias
Regina Peruggi
Steven Pinker
George Plimpton
Letty Cottin Pogrebin
Roman Polanski
Reynolds Price
W. V. Quine
Nahid Rachlin
Dan Rather
James Redfield
Lynn Redgrave
Leni Riefenstahl
Joan Rivers
Graham Robb
Ned Rorem
A. M. Rosenthal
Jack Rosenthal
Henry Rosovsky

Wilbur Ross
Howard Rubenstein
William Ruddick
Oliver Sacks
Edward Said
Sebastiao Salgado
Harrison Salisbury
Stephen Sandy
Francesco Scavullo
Mary Schmidt-Campbell
Robert Schuller
Glenn Seaborg
Wilfrid Sheed
Cybill Shepherd
Alix Kates Shulman
John Simon
Jane Smiley
Alexander McCall Smith
Albert Solnit
Nicholas Sparks
Gloria Steinem
Robert J. Sternberg
Fred Mustard Stewart
Catharine R. Stimpson
Leo Stone
Mark Strand
Whitley Strieber
Elizabeth Strong-Cuevas
Miguel Syjuco
Gay Talese
Maria Tallchief
Amy Tan
Lionel Tiger
Joseph F. Traub
Laurence H. Tribe
Alan Trustman

Desmond M. Tutu
John Updike
Andrew Vachss
Sander Vanocur
Gwen Verdon
Patricia Volk
David Foster Wallace
Tom Wallace
Wendy Wasserstein
Carol Weston
Nancy Willard
Edward O. Wilson
Gahan Wilson
Frank Wilczeck
Hilma Wolitzer
Stuart Woods
Paul Zindel
William Zinsser
Elmo R. Zumwalt, Jr.

Floyd Abrams
(New York attorney, partner, Cahill, Gordon & Reindell)

My favorite word is "iguana."

Diane Ackerman
(Best-selling author, *A Natural History of the Senses*; *One Hundred Names for Love*)

"Hapax legemonon" is one of my favorites. We are unique if we endure. I also like "sanctity" and "holy." I am not a theist, however, I'm an earth-ecstatic.

Rob Ackerman
(Playwright; *Origin of the Species*; *Tabletop*; *Disconnect*; *Volleygirls*)

"Monkey."

Hanan Al-Shaykh
(Author, *The Story of Zahra*)

Washwasha. It means "a whisper" in Arabic, and it sounds exactly like a whisper.

"Reminiscent." Whenever I hear it, I visualize two delicate hands trying to pick up things. Maybe this image has to do with the word *rammaser* in French.

"Frangipani." Whenever I hear it, I smell my childhood. In Beirut, my neighborhood was full of frangipani trees.

"Err." Like an animal sound.

"Fascination." It was my first English word I like to remember after it was repeated over and over in the film *Love in the Afternoon* since Audrey Hepburn was my idol only because she gave me confidence; to be slim is all right and even complimentary in a society which considers it a drawback. After seeing the film, I kept asking what does the word "fascination" mean, to no avail, until I became seventeen years old. I thought

I was superior; I could speak English; I could say "fantastic," "fantasy," "fantasia," and "fascination."

Muhammad Ali
(Three-time World Heavyweight Champion Boxer)
"The Greatest!"

Norman Arnoff
(New York Attorney and columnist for
The New York Law Journal)

"Justice"

Justice Benjamin Cardozo in *The Nature of the Judicial Process* wrote: "Justice is a concept far more subtle and indefinite than mere obedience to a rule. It remains to some extent when all is said and done a synonym of aspiration, a mood of exaltation, a yearning for what is fine or high."

Aristotle, in regard to the meaning of equity and justice as those terms were applicable in arbitration, wrote (and which was posted on the wall of an arbitration hearing room at the New York Stock Exchange): "Equity is justice in that goes beyond the written law, and it is equitable to prefer arbitration to the law court, for the arbitrator keeps equity in view, whereas the judge looks only to the law and the reason why arbitrators were appointed is that equity might prevail."

Justice Benjamin Cardozo again, in an address to a Columbia University Law School graduating class, stated: "How it lies with you to uplift what is low, erase what is false, and redeem what is lost till all the world shall see and seeing understand that union of the scholar's thought, the Knights ardor, the hero's passion and the mystic's yearning which in its best moments of self expression is the spirit of the bar." Justice Cardozo's definition of justice and his understanding of the concept of justice is that it is a term of aspiration which motivates lawyers (especially lawyers), jurors, and judges to do what is morally right and fair

when the text of the law is not a clear guide. More often than not the law is not clear.

In thinking about what I do as a lawyer and my role as an "Officer of the Court," I have expressed that "the practice of law is the practice of justice." The terminology and meaning of "Officer of the Court" also represents our aspirations in that the lawyer internalizes the law and takes it with him in contexts outside the courthouse. Justice and a lawyer's ethics should govern the lawyer even outside of court. The term "Officer of the Court" is the broadest reach of the law also giving the concept and term of justice its broadest meaning.

Once in a case in Suffolk County just before a client was going to give up in a case involving fire safety regulations in respect to a hotel where fire safety was the issue and the case seemed to be fixed against my client and his investors, I said: "Law is the conscience of man, and conscience is the eye of God" (i.e., sometimes there is more in pursuing a case than one's client's interest or the interest of the lawyer). Justice and similar concepts motivate those who participate in the legal process to interpret and apply the law to achieve the highest standards of morality and fairness.

Once I was assigned to represent in Federal Court a lookout for drug dealers in the South Bronx. My client's role was to walk the dividing line on the street and warn his coconspirators when the police and DEA came. My client jumped bail and skipped out after the first day of trial, which lasted for a week. For four days I was sitting next to an empty chair. The evidence was thin against my client. In summation to prevent the jury's adverse inference because of my client's flight, I declared to the jury: "My client is not in the courthouse but justice is." Hopefully for every lawyer, justice is always in and outside of the courthouse, whatever the context.

John Ashbery
(Poet, *Planisphere*; *Flow Chart*;
Self-Portrait in a Convex Mirror)

My favorite words are "climate," "meretricious," and "intermittent." I wonder what it all means …

Margaret Atwood
(Booker Prize-winning author, *The Blind Assassin*;
The Handmaiden's Tale; *Cat's Eye*; *The Robber Bride*)

Here are my words:

Thirty years ago, my favorite words were "chthonic" and "igneous." (I was in my Precambrian Shield phase.) Then they became "jungoid," "musilagenous," and "larval" (biology took over). Right now they are "diaphanous" and "lunar." The latter especially, as it combines rock and light, solidity and inaccessibility, with a suggestion of tidal activity, and howling wolves.

Nicholson Baker
(Author, *U & I: A True Story*; *Vox*; *Checkpoint*)

Of abstract nouns containing the letter *l*, my favorites are "reluctance" and "revulsion."

The "luct" in "reluctance" functions as an oral brake or clutch ("clutch" and "luct" being sonic kin), making the word seem politely hesitant, tactful, circumspect—willing to let the hired tongue have its fun before completing its meaning.

My uncle tried to teach me how to say "revulsion" properly when I was five: under his tutelage the second syllable became a kind of Shakespearean dry heave. The word is full of exuberant, *l*-raising relish and revelry.

The first word I liked was "broom."

Russell Baker
(Former PBS host, *Masterpiece Theatre*; former columnist, *The New York Times*)

"Melancholy" is one of my favorite words, but if proper nouns may be considered, no word satisfies me more utterly than "Pushtunistan." Can you bear a fardel? The funniest word in English is "fardel," the most pompous is "obloquy," the most unnecessary is "congeries," and the hardest to pronounce without sounding like a twit is "prescient."

David Baldacci
(Author, *Absolute Power*; *Total Control*; *One Summer*)

I know that some people say that I use a lot of the same verbs ... My verbs tend to be very active like "plunged" or "hurtled" or words like that. I like the fast pace and the action, but with *Total Control* I tried to delve more into the emotional side, and some of the words there are more tender words. You're trying to describe how a character is actually feeling.

I guess I'm a fan of most of the words that I employ in my books. I can't say that I have any particular favorites. It's hard just working over and over trying to say something the right way, for exactly what you're trying to say at that moment in time. And you could probably always go back and second-guess yourself about it. But at some point you just have to say at this point in my life and this point in time this is the best I can do with this, and then you have to move on. With a word, it's kind of an endless choice. Sometimes you hit it and sometimes you don't.

Dave Barry

(Syndicated columnist, humorist)

I am very partial to "weasel." It's hard to imagine a thought that wouldn't be improved by the addition of a "weasel." For example:

Weak: "Spiro Agnew was vice president from 1969 through 1973."

Better: "Spiro Agnew was vice president from 1969 through 1973. What a weasel." Another excellent word is *qua* because most people (me, for example) have no idea what it means. So *qua* tends to lend an air of unchallengeable authority to a statement.

Weak: "The Mets suck."

Better: "The Mets *qua* Mets suck."

And of course you can't go wrong with "sputum."

John Barth

(National Book Award–winning author, *Chimera*;
The Sot-Weed Factor; *Once Upon a Time*)

Pet Words

I can no more name a favorite word than choose a favorite food: so many, and of such differing varieties of appeal, that to rank them is to compare ... apples and oranges. All the same, three pet categories, if not pet words, come to mind:

- Certain Latinate adjectives of decidedly poetical sound but (in my working vocabulary, at least) insufficiently certain sense for me to deploy them comfortably. *Lambent. Plangent. Crepuscular.* I have contrived to publish upwards of three thousand narrative pages without, I think, ever before now describing anything in God's creation or mine as either lambent, plangent, or crepuscular. To my ear such hyper-evocotives are—how to put it? Too lambent, perhaps. Too plangent. Too crepuscular.

- Certain adverbs and prepositions of a particularly rough-poetic air, the virtual contrary of Category One. *Akimbo. Athwart. Doggo.* What a doughty, vintage-English way to position one's arms; to set a plank (there's a handsome word, too); to simply sprawl (and there's another).

- Certain Greek imports with clustered consonants and/or diphthongs (e.g., *diphthong*) tantalizing to the Anglophonic tongue and ear. *Rhythms,* for starters, and *mnemonic, chthonic,* and *phthisis,* once you're in the spirit of it; also that standby from our childhood chemistry sets, *phenolphthalein*—especially the busy stretch between the *o* and the *a* of that reagent. But it's a homely native English fraction that holds my unofficial Guinness record for the longest unbroken string of consonantal spits and sputters. Pronounce carefully the simple word *sixths,* and you'll hear the vexed-pussycat sound of no fewer than four unvowelled hisses: the *k* plus *s* of *x*, the thornish *th*, and the sign-off sibilant.

Sixths: yes.

Kenneth Battelle
(World-renowned hairdresser, Kenneth of Kenneth's Salon)

I think the three-letter words that end in *ex*—"hex," "Mex," "rex," "sex," "Tex," "vex"—are amazing as they conjure so much of a sense of power and are so descriptive.

I love "curmudgeon," as I would like to be one. Maybe I am. And I love "dichotomy," as I find the world to be just one big one.

Julie Baumgold
(Author, *Creatures of Habit*; *The Diamond*)

"Night," because the night forgives, it keeps secrets, cloaks the bad things of the day, hides ugliness, because you feel you can pass through it invisibly, because the people of the night see more in the shield of darkness. Almost any word sounds better

to me with "night" in front of or behind it and the best word of all is "tonight." As Dracula said, "Listen to them—the children of the night. What sweet music they make."

William Baumol
(Economist, NYU)

My favorite words are "chutzpah," "ambiguity," and "chimera." The word "chutzpah," which can't even be spelled properly, much less translated fully, from the Yiddish is perhaps *primus inter pares* among the trove of Yiddish words rich in nuance and content. Meaning a compound of audacity and sheer gall, all carried out with panache, competence, and a touch of humor, there seems to be no substitute in any other language.

"Ambiguity" is one of my favorites because I consider it to be the crucial attribute of any work of art that has any prospect of enduring. Good examples are the Bach cantatas, which, after all, were prepared as pieces of Lutheran propaganda. If their content were unambiguous, would they still attract the many Oriental musicians who perform them so superbly, and to whom their Lutheran origins can mean very little?

"Chimera" recommends itself to me because I just like the sound and like the concept. Does it need more justification than that?

Orson Bean
(Actor, *Desperate Housewives*; *Dr. Quinn, Medicine Woman*; humorist, author)

"Belly button" is the word.

I love it because it makes me laugh and because it collects belly button "lint," for which there is no known use. We need more totally useless things in life.

Ira Berkow
(Pulitzer Prize-winning sports reporter and columnist,
The New York Times)

My offering for favorite word is "bamboozle." The sound of the word gives instant delight, and brings a smile to one's face, unless of course you yourself have been bamboozled, or the target of a bamboozle—that is, tricked, cheated, or conned. I looked up the derivation and the dictionary says "obscure origins," which adds to the joy. It obviously was invented because we needed such a juicy word. The happy placing of the pair of *b*'s, the twin *o*'s, the earthy *m*, the lurking *l*, and the zippy *z* provide a word of nonpareil pronunciation. You can say it with the long *boo*—"bamboooozle"—or with a kind of Yiddish accent, giving the *oo*'s a softer, tighter, bosomy sound.

To be sure, there are numerous words in our rich mother tongue that are a pleasure to let roll from our lips. But when asked to select my favorite word, it was "bamboozle" that first popped into mind. Why, I don't know. I rarely use the word, so it must simply have been lying in wait in my subconscious to spring up at this very moment. And since I believe it is usually sound advice to stick to initial instincts, I do so now with this luscious and loony word.

Anne Bernays
(Author, *Trophy House*; *Professor Romeo*)

Nice of you to ask me about my favorite words. Here they are, four of them.

"Eighty-seven." In my family this is a generic number meaning "many." As in "When I went to get my driver's license renewed, there were eighty-seven people waiting in line in front of me." Or "This is the eighty-seventh time this week I've asked you to clean up the mess in your room." Justin claims that it probably derives from Lincoln's Gettysburg Address—"Fourscore and seven years ago ..."—but I'm doubtful. In any case, eighty-seven is an all-purpose number, making a clear statement. It's very useful.

My other three words—"fat," "old," "conceited"—belong together and are examples of the kind of straight language I admire and mourn the loss of. All are routinely euphemized, as in "obese," "overweight," "husky," "aging," "elderly," and some form of (yuck) "senior citizen," "narcissistic," "entitled," "self-absorbed." Why can't we call things by their true names?

Sven Birkerts

(Essayist, author, *The Gutenberg Elegies*)

Favorite words ... I've been going about for days now tilting my head and blinking as the candidates have it out in the cranial arena, and I've decided that it's too hard to choose from an unlimited field. Why not just stab the dictionary with a knife like the Dadaists did? But no, the better solution is to impose a constraint. Mine? I will select, somewhat at random, a small crop of beauts from Malcolm Lowry's *Under the Volcano*. Because this novel, about the last day in the life of Geoffrey Firmin— drunkard, consul—once intoxicated me as no cruder distillation has ever managed. I'm not sure I could ever explain the process, the chemical transaction, but I will say that Lowry, even more than Joyce or Woolf, infected me with his obvious love for distinct words—for their look, their sound, their suggestiveness, as well as for the way they jostle together in a line of print, seducing the eye-beam, playing crack-the-whip down in the recesses of the ear. An homage, then, a *sortes Lowriae*:

plangent, sculpturings, lacquered, naphtha, waxplants, spoliation, mescal, thaumaturgy, coquelicot, casuistry, strychnine, whiskerando, Pleiades, anis, jai-alai, abbatoir, plantains, dolorous, bougainvillea, chamois, thrumming, horripilating, multitudinously, exacerbated, cobalt, hippodrome, rajah, toothmug, antipodes, gesticulations, barranca, parapet, mirador, runcible, monarchical, immedicable, pariah, convulvulus, pyramidal, cashiered, dementia, pulque, sulfurously, bedraggedly, honeymoon, calvados, digestif, mestizo, Palladium, mosque, bobolink, jocosely, confetti, assuaged, orchestras, elastic, borracho, confederate, pocketing, ventilated, pandemonium.

Bruce Bliven
(Editor and writer, *The New Yorker*)

By far my favorite word is "cat." I know how to spell it. As the product of what was known as a "progressive school" in the 1920s, I can spell only a handful of words with equal assurance. And in addition, I have enjoyed a personal relationship with at least one cat, and more often two cats, almost all of my life. I have learned, as a result, that two cats are easier than one because some of the outrageous demands a cat makes are directed to the other cat rather than to his or her person. I've liked the cats I've known well, and I wish I'd had the chance to know some of their family (*Felidae*) members better, especially lions, tigers, leopards, jaguars, cougars, wildcats, lynx, and cheetahs. And next to "cat" as a noun, perhaps my second favorite is "cat" as a prefix. I like catfish, catsup, and catalogs, although I am not especially fond of caterpillars. Above all—this paragraph reminds me—I am categorically devoted to catnaps.

Naomi Bliven
(Book reviewer, *The New Yorker*)

Though there are many things that I like very much (chocolate, for instance), the words for my favorite things aren't favorite words. In fact, I think I dislike favorite words—especially other people's favorite words. Remember the years when every writer accused everybody else of "hubris?" And when reviewers called every okay performance an epiphany? Years ago I tried to float a comparatively unfamiliar word, "vatic," to see how far it would go, but my editor immediately changed it to "prophetic." After "irenic" was changed to "ironic," I decided to accept the limitations of other people's vocabularies. My favorite words are words everybody knows.

Lawrence Block

(Edgar Award-winning mystery writer,
Burglars Can't Be Choosers)

I'm the least bit reluctant to name my favorite words. I need them all, you see, and wouldn't want to hurt the feelings of those I omit. Nonetheless, I've come up with three.

"Philtrum" is a favorite. It's that vertical groove that bisects the upper lip, and much of my delight in it stems from the mere fact that such a word exists. What anonymous wordsmith, rubbing his own philtrum with his forefinger, decided the thing ought to have a name? And how did he name it philtrum? The word seems all wrong for the job; if it's a part of the body at all, and not a secret potion or a riddle, it ought to be located somewhere in the kidney.

There's a Jewish legend explaining the origin, not of the word, but of the philtrum itself. Before you were born, you see, an angel sat down with you and told you the meaning of life and all the secrets of the universe. And then he put his forefinger right there and gave a shove, hard enough to leave a permanent indentation in your upper lip, and you forgot everything he told you. What I forgot, over and over for twenty or thirty years, is the word itself; I kept having to learn it anew. Maybe that's why I'm so uncommonly fond of it now.

A second favorite word is "irenic." I don't believe I've ever typed it before, and I'm certain I've never uttered it aloud. It became a favorite when I read how someone had taken the lexicophagous William F. Buckley to task for using words nobody else knows. For example, he was asked, just what did irenic mean? It meant peaceful, Buckley replied. So why not say peaceful? I wanted the extra syllable, Buckley explained.

I liked that. There are lots of times I want an extra syllable. Life being what it is, I don't even get to use the word peaceful all that much, let alone irenic. But someday when we're all sitting around the campfire singing "Goodnight, Irene," maybe I'll get my chance.

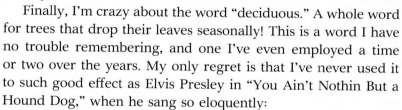

Finally, I'm crazy about the word "deciduous." A whole word for trees that drop their leaves seasonally! This is a word I have no trouble remembering, and one I've even employed a time or two over the years. My only regret is that I've never used it to such good effect as Elvis Presley in "You Ain't Nothin But a Hound Dog," when he sang so eloquently:

"Deciduous high class, but that was just a lie ..."

Roy Blount, Jr.
(Humorist, author, *Crackers*; *What Men Don't Tell Women*;
Roy Blount's Book of Southern Humor; *Hail, Hail, Euphoria!*)

I was actually asked this question once on a radio show: "You're an author, what's your favorite word?"

At first I was nonplussed. "Well," I said, "there are so many nice words ..." Then I said, "Chicken." That was years ago. I have had ample time to reconsider. I still say, "Chicken."

It's funny, it's wholesome, it has a life of its own.

My favorite sentence (though it isn't complete) is "Chicken in the bread pan, pecking up dough."

Tom Bodett
(Voice of Motel 6; author, *The Free-Fall of Webster Cummings*)

I like strings of words. And then there's just the sounds of words that sound like what they are. The word "pester." Have you ever had somebody pester you? It sounds exactly like what it is. It's a wonderful word to say.

T. Coraghessan Boyle
(Award-winning author, *East Is East*; *World's End*;
When the Killing's Done)

My favorite word (of the moment, anyway) is "steatopygia," which refers to "excessive fatness of the hips and buttocks, especially as found among the Hottentots and certain other African tribes, particularly among the women" (*Webster's New*

Twentieth Century Dictionary, unabridged, second edition). I first came across the term during my research for *Water Music,* and I liked the idea of this evolutionary holdover—the fat so stored could be drawn upon by the depleted system in times of drought and duress. (A certain Seattle rapper has made his reputation on a song testifying to the usefulness and beauty of this adaptation, by the way.) For me, of course, the term has special significance too, beyond its use in my African novel and its splendid display in the flesh on our streets today, as I myself have inherited very little in the way of additional flesh from my ancestors. In fact, my own buttocks can be said to be entirely "nugatory."

Ray Bradbury
(Science-fiction author, *The Martian Chronicles;*
Dandelion Wine)

My two words are "ramshackle" and "cinnamon."

It's hard to explain why "ramshackle" has played such a part in my writing. I've found myself using it in essays and stories to describe certain situations which, I suppose, are part of all of our lives. Half the time we feel we are ramshackle people, lopsided, no right or left side of the brain, with some terrible vacuum in between. That, to me, is ramshackle. The way we lead our lives; my life is a litter of junk around my office, which has driven my wife and children mad. If anyone is ramshackle, it is yours truly.

The word "cinnamon" derives, I suppose, from visiting my grandma's pantry when I was a kid. I loved to read the labels on the spice boxes; curries from far places in India and cinnamons from across the world. The word causes me to think of voyages and ships on the sea and the Arabian Nights. I've used it in books such as *The Martian Chronicles* and many other stories. I find that over the years, I have to go back and take it out of stories because I've used it too often. One of the last times was in describing a wild Hollywood character, Constance Rattigan,

in my novel *A Graveyard for Lunatics,* in which I describe her basic color as cinnamon. I don't seem to be able to give up on the word.

Barbara Taylor Bradford
(Best-selling author, *A Woman Of Substance*; *Playing The Game*)

My favorite word is "gormless." It means stupid, dull, dull-witted. I've used it in *A Woman Of Substance* and in all of my Yorkshire novels.

Rosanno Brazzi
(Actor, *South Pacific*; *The Barefoot Contessa*)

How could I say I "love" if I did not know the "word."

Joe Bob Briggs
(Humorist, author, *A Guide to Western Civilization, or My Story*; *Profoundly Disturbing: Shocking Movies that Changed History*)

The most beautiful word I ever heard is *estacionamiento.* It's Spanish. After I learned to say it elegantly, musically, I found out what it means: parking lot.

Helen Gurley Brown
(International editor, *Cosmopolitan*)

My favorite words are "comprehensive," "unilateral," and "reciprocity." I don't know why I use them so much—I don't even *like* them. There are so many more beautiful words such as "rhapsody," exquisite," "indigenous," and "tranquil," but I never *use* them. Using the favorite threesome must make me feel important or something.

Mario Buatta
(Interior designer)

My favorite word is "Dinner is served!"

Edna Buchanan
(Pulitzer Prize-winning columnist and best-selling author of Miami crime novels)

Amok, *berserk*, and *bizarre* are sentimental favorites from my years of covering crime for the *Miami Herald*. I delighted in seeing how many times I could work them into the newspaper each day, despite editors dedicated to keeping them out.

Amok is short, but few four-letter words evoke such red-faced, wild-eyed imagery. *Berserk* is a hard-edged hatchet blow of a word, deliciously ominous when spoken aloud. Not surprisingly, both hatchet and berserk were often companion pieces in the same sentence. Civic-minded editors tried, but were unable to ban *bizarre* from the newspaper. So much of the time it is the only possible word to describe certain events on Miami's steamy streets.

Leo Buscaglia
(Psychologist, author; *Living, Loving & Learning*)

What a delightful idea ... a book of favorite words! Everyone who works/plays with words each day has such a list. Words that choke, that soothe, that frustrate, that delight, that stimulate.

As for those that tickle my ear, may I start with "love," "rapture," "ecstasy" (which also tickle my heart) and "frump," "quagmire," "phlegm," "loquacious," and "malleable," which sound and look delightfully goofy to me, and tickle my fancy.

Thanks for including me in the fun.

A. S. Byatt

(Booker Prize-winning author, *Possession: A Romance*;
The Matisse Stories; *The Children's Book*)

My favorite words tend to be colour words. At the moment I'm very keen on vermillion, which I think is a very beautiful word, or emerald. Or I like the sort of words that go running along like Shakespeare saying the "multitudinous seas incarnadine making the green one red." And I like the thing English can do as sort of sitting one of those very long words next to a very short word. And I like what I learned at school about the mixture of putting long Latin words next to very short Anglo-Saxon words, incarnadine next to red, which is what Milton did so well. He knew how to play the Germanic side of English off against the Latin side. So really I like almost all words.

Jeanne Cavelos

(Author, *The Many Faces of Van Helsing*; director, Odyssey
Fantasy Writing Workshop)

I've had different favorite words at different times in my life. When I was little, I delighted in saying "doy" or "chunk of dough." Those words still make me laugh.

These days, I have two favorites. I love the word "faux." I first really learned to appreciate this word watching the home-shopping channels, which addicted me for many months. In their glamorous parlance, vinyl became faux leather and cut glass became faux diamonds. The word itself is deceptive; it doesn't look the way it sounds. And when you insert it before a noun, that noun ends up taking on the exact opposite meaning.

My other favorite word is "irritant." Captain Kirk of *Star Trek* brought this word to my attention when he called someone an irritant. There are so many irritants in our lives—long lines at the grocery store, television news anchors, telephone salespeople—and sometimes I get very aggravated. But if I can just say (or scream), "This is an irritant!" it makes me feel better.

The feel of the word in my mouth, the sound of it, brings me joy. And then everything's okay.

Go figure!

Ben Cheever
(Author, *The Plagiarist*; *The First Dog*)

At first I thought my favorite word was "adroit" because of the way it sounds, and because I'm not.

But then I remembered that when my first son first went to school, he came back with two new words. These were "no" and "mine."

Both good, but if I had to choose a single syllable, above all others, it would have to be "yes." I know it doesn't sound like much. Or rather it sounds like something a snake might do. But meaning's got to count for something. Besides it's simple, elegant, and so rarely heard.

Susan Cheever
(Author, *Looking for Work*; *A Woman's Life*;
American Bloombsbury)

My favorite words are "yes" and "no." They are the us-words, the words that say it all. I love them for their completeness, their simplicity, and their appropriateness to all occasions. Are they not, after all, the most powerful words we have? Yes?

Ron Chernow
(Pulitzer Prize-winning biographer, *Washington: A Life*;
National Book Award–winning author, *The House of Morgan*;
The Warburgs; *Alexander Hamilton*)

To the unsuspecting reader, the writer's life seems a monkish and solitary one, a dryly monotonous grind. Every writer has encountered the cocktail party platitude, "You must be *very* disciplined." "On the contrary," I always reply, "I am completely

out of control. If you must know, I have far more trouble stopping than starting."

We writers are closet hedonists, luxuriating in a wilderness of words. Words shower down upon us like manna, gratifying the senses as much by what our imaginations impart as by the secret flavors they contain. I confess a partiality to words that titillate several senses at once—juicy, rounded, succulent words that swell in the mouth and burst like overripe fruit. Words that vibrate with color, beauty, and intensity, expressing the plenitude of life: brilliant, vivid, exquisite, luscious, gorgeous, and voluptuous. Certain clusters of words seem to fascinate me: engaging, enchanting, enthralling; shine, sheen, shimmer, shadow; bewitching, bedizened, bedazzled. I fervently await the day that opalescent or adamantine will suddenly arise as *le mot juste* in a paragraph. Since cheating is forbidden upon pain of expulsion from the craft, I may have to wait decades just to unsheathe these two fancy words.

In short, nobody should pity writers their spare, ascetic lives. For while the world goes about its more serious work, we sit hunched over our word processors, far from view, reveling in our own secret world of musical sounds. Bet you didn't expect to hear this, Frumkes, from a so-called business historian?

Mary Higgins Clark
(Best-selling author, *Remember Me*; *Loves Music, Loves to Dance*; *I'll Walk Alone*)

My favorite word is "memories." It always brings back the glad and sad of all the yesterdays, the salad days, the solemn and hilarious days, the bitter and the sweet days, the hectic and the neat days. "Memories," the word. That is the DNA of a writer!

Arthur C. Clarke

(Science-fiction writer, *2001: A Space Odyssey*;
Childhood's End)

"Incarnadine" (from *Macbeth*) is one of my favorites, but I seldom have a chance to use it!

So I'll settle for "Serendib" or "Serendip" and its derivatives—because I live here! I've even used it in a book title: *The View from Serendip*.

> Serendip (or Serendib) is one of the many ancient names of Ceylon; it derives from the Muslim traders' Sarandib. The Greeks and Romans called the island Taprobane: the indigenous name was Sri Lanka ("the Resplendent Land"), and since 1972 this has been its official designation, though the national airline is still Air Ceylon, and no one ever talks of Sri Lanka tea.

From *The View From Serendip* (Random House)

James Clavell

(Author, *Shogun*; *Noble House*)

My favorite words ... "Once upon a time ..."

Hillary Rodham Clinton

(United States Secretary of State)

"Love."

Michael Connelly

(Edgar Award–winning author, *The Black Echo*; *The Scarecrow*;
In the Shadow of the Master; *The Drop*)

I don't know if it's that I was influenced by Steve McQueen in
Bullet, but Harry Bosch is relentless as a bullet. He's a man of
few words. He reacts by nodding, so "nodding" ends up in all
my books. I had an editor who pointed out that Harry nods too
much. In fact in one book he nodded 243 times.

Denton A. Cooley

(Cardiac surgeon)

The word "eleemosynary" is one which I find useful when
referring to charitable purposes. I find the word "paradigm"
also useful.

Frequently I refer to success vs. failure and victory vs.
defeat.

Wes Craven

(Film writer/director, *A Nightmare on Elm Street*; *Scream*)

Here's my answer, three months later, to your query about my
favorite word. Sorry for the delay, but three trips to Europe,
four scripts, and a TV pilot kinda got in the way.

All of which should lead up to my favorite word being
"procrastinate," although it's actually one of my *least* favorite
words—probably because I've always felt it described so many
of my actions so terribly well.

Anyway, my favorite word? "Plangent." I just think it's such
a wonderfully evocative and elegant word. In second place I'd
have to put "squinch," which is a sort of corbeling, but every
time I use it, people think I'm making it up!

Quentin Crisp
(Author, *The Naked Civil Servant*)

I make every effort *not* to have a favorite word. I find that, if I write carelessly, I later have to delete the word "extraordinary" several times from each page, which must mean that I use it often in my heart but I couldn't say that it—or any—particular word is a "favorite." I'm not sure that I know what the word means. Isn't it a sin to have a favorite word?

Mr. Graves said:

> Words repeated over and over
> till the sense sickens in them and all but dies—
> these The Great Devil, tenderly as a lover,
> will lay his hand upon and hypnotise.

Norm Crosby
(Comedian)

My word is "apocryphal," and it comes from a nursery rhyme: "Sing a song of sixpence apocryphal of rye," etc.

Also, I like: "acrylic"—someone who reviews shows!

"Romance"—like, if you had a picnic in a Roman park, you'd probably find ... "Sacrament"—the capital of California—and "cabaret"—a hat worn by a French taxi driver!

Mario Cuomo
(Former governor of the state of New York)

My favorite word is one I made up. *Insinuendo.* It combines the power of insinuation with that of innuendo.

Clive Cussler
(Author, *Raise the Titanic; Inca Gold; Devil's Gate*)

I love to end a chapter by making something or someone disappear "as though they never existed."

Then the trick is, where in hell do you go from there??

Scott Daspin
(Managing director, head of sales, Convergex)

My favorite words are *monomaniacal*, *bibliomaniacal*, and *hypnagogic*. I like *aplomb*, too.

Olivia de Havilland
(Actress, *The Snake Pit*; *The Heiress*)

I understand your preoccupation with words and am charmed by the various examples which your letter cited. I am myself attracted by almost any French word—written or spoken: all those *aux, eux*, and *eaux* are so beautiful to read and so lovely to hear. Before I knew its meaning, I thought *saucisson* so exquisite that it seemed the perfect name to give a child—until I learned it meant sausage!

Len Deighton
(Mystery writer, *The IPCRESS File*; *Catch a Falling Spy*)

"Grace."

Not only does it sound as smooth as silk, but the word's meanings extend from attractive (appearance), through willingness and musical frolics and special on-campus terms, to its use as an aristocratic title. And it has special religious significance, too. Don't listen to me—look it up in a big dictionary. It's a fine word.

Oscar de la Renta
(Fashion designer)

My favorite word is "yes" because I'm a positive person.

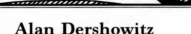

Alan Dershowitz

(Harvard professor of law, criminal attorney, author)

I always loved the phrase "and yet." I was reading Elie Wiesel's autobiography and he said "and yet" was one of his favorite words. I love ironic phrases. I love turns of phrase. There are certain words that come out of my Talmudic tradition that are hard to translate. For example, when I studied Talmud there was a word, *khal v'chomir*, which means "from the simple to the difficult," perhaps "a fortiori" would be a rough translation. For a lawyer that's a very valuable concept, and I often find it hard to put into words. But I love language, I love the art of writing. For me the art of writing is, of all the things I do in my life, the most satisfying. I don't own a typewriter or a computer. I use spiral pads and felt pens, and I write a million words a year by hand.

Phyllis Diller

(Comic, entertainer, TV personality

I love words like "aurora borealis." I see pastel colors in my mind's eye when I think of that word. I adore words like "ephemeral," "mellifluous," "diaphanous," "glissando," "whispering," and "shimmering." These are a few of my favorite words. They ripple forward softly, suggesting music and beauty.

In my work as a stand-up comic, I must use monosyllabic words, ugly shock words. The operative joke word must end the gag and hopefully be a one-syllable word ending with an explosive consonant as in "butt."

"Agamemnon," "Beelzebub," "lollipop," and "Mississippi" are funny words.

"Plague," "torture," and "bomb" are terrifying words.

"Antidisestablishmentarianism" is a long word.

"Sweet, precious, darling" are loving words.

Words are wonderful. They are the playthings of the mind.

Rita Dove

(Pulitzer Prize-winning poet and novelist,
Through the Ivory Gate)

A favorite word from my childhood is "ragamuffin." Oh, how I loved the shaggy-dog compactness of this word. It applied to my favorite after-school program, *The Little Rascals,* ragamuffins every one (except the boringly cute Darla); and I thought of it every time we had corn muffins for Sunday breakfast, warm and golden and crumbly. Whenever my parents used the word "ragamuffin" to instill shame in me, I smiled secretly and felt vindicated, inviolate in my essential child-ness.

A more adult preference came with university life and an understanding of irony at its bone-deepest level—that is, the irony between the sound of a word and its meaning. For me, "barbiturate" exemplified this dichotomy: what a delicious, seductive word, beautiful and inviting with its softened *t*'s and shooshy, shifting center. How ironic, then, that our culture has reduced its thrust to a convenient pharmaceutical!

Roddy Doyle

(Booker Prize-winning author,
Paddy Clarke Ha, Ha, Ha; The Dead Republic)

When I was writing *Paddy Clarke*, the word "brilliant" kept appearing again and again and again, because it's very common in Dublin. It's a word I've used myself quite a lot having grown up in Dublin. It just arises in conversation very quickly. I'm not sure if it's a personal favorite. I don't actually listen to myself too often.

Dame Margaret Drabble
(Author, *The Realms of Gold*)

On this occasion I will select as my favorite word "squirrel." This is partly because I like the elegant little creature itself, and have a fondness for words with the somewhat neglected letter *q* in them. Also, I have a slight difficulty in pronouncing the letter *r*; but my husband rolls an *r* beautifully, and I try to encourage him to speak of squirrels whenever an opportunity arises. This is quite often as he, too, is fond of them and can easily be enticed to speak of them. We have them in the garden and we can hear them playing noisily on the bedroom roof. These are gray squirrels, not the almost-vanished native British red ones, but we like gray ones, too, and deplore the habit of redescribing them as tree rats in order to discourage affection for them.

The very fact that one can arouse hostility to a squirrel by calling it a rat shows the power of the Word. It is a small but significant illustration of how we can manipulate or be manipulated by language. Why should we feel free to poison a rat but not a squirrel?

Perhaps I should say a word, too, in favor of Beatrix Potter's fine story *Squirrel Nutkin,* in my view her masterpiece. I look forward to reading this to my grandchildren.

Dominick Dunne
(Author, *The Two Mrs. Grenvilles*; *An Inconvenient Woman*)

As a born people watcher, I have always been drawn to the word "riveted" when applied to people's behavior. "I was riveted." It could mean that I was either fascinated or appalled by the behavior, but more important, it means that I was utterly absorbed in the viewing of it.

I also like the word "swell," either as an adjective or a noun. In my youth, it was slang, frowned upon by teachers. But now, in its adjective usage, it is to me a perfect word to describe approval of someone or something. As a noun, I like to use it to describe an upper-class person of impeccable lineage and

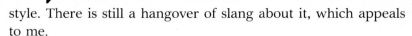

style. There is still a hangover of slang about it, which appeals to me.

In my novel, *A Season in Purgatory,* I searched and searched for a word to describe an emotional feeling that one character has for another. It was not love. It was not obsession. It was more than fascination. Finally, I hit upon the word "transfixed." It was perfect for my purposes. I have grown deeply attached to it. My Chapter One ends with these sentences:

> Transfixed. What an odd word. Was I transfixed with Constant Bradley? Yes I was. I was completely transfixed by Constant Bradley.

Andrea Dworkin
(Author, feminist)

I like the word "autumn," probably because I like the season, but also because I like the silent *n*.

I like the words "lambent" and "poignant," although I never use them.

I particularly like the words "earth," "wind," "dust," "ash," "dark," "sad," and I use them often.

Freeman Dyson
(Professor of physics, The Institute for Advanced Study, Princeton University; author, *Disturbing The Universe*.)

Dear Lewis Frumkes,

I just came back from three weeks of travel and found your message waiting. I am not a logophile and try always to use words that are short and simple. Instead of giving you a quote from my own writing, I give you a quote from Leo Szilard, a great scientist who was also a great human being. He was dissatisfied with the commandments of Moses and wrote a new set of ten commandments to replace them. Here are the last two of his commandments:

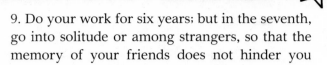

9. Do your work for six years; but in the seventh, go into solitude or among strangers, so that the memory of your friends does not hinder you from being what you have become.

10. Lead your life with a gentle hand and be ready to leave whenever you are called.

Szilard wrote his commandments in German. This English translation is by Jacob Bronowski.

I look forward to seeing what the other contributors have written.

Yours sincerely,
Freeman Dyson

Fernanda Eberstadt
(Author, *Low Tide*; *The Furies*; granddaughter of Ogden Nash)

I like the density of nouns fresh-minted into verbs. In his poem "Maud," Tennyson describers a snotty boy's stare "Gorgonizing me from head to foot." Or, a friend to his wife when she gets in a panic, "Quit hamster-wheeling."

Paul Edwards
(Philosopher, editor, *The Encyclopedia of Philosophy*)

Here are some of my favorite words. I have been collecting them during the last few weeks. It is quite a long list and at the end I will try to explain what I like about them:

bamboozle, pulverize, flamboyance, irretrievable, unflappable, unpalatable, rambunctious, gibberish, modulate, promulgate, convoluted (as in convoluted style), unadulterated balderdash, hodgepodge, mishmash, pussyfoot, gobbledygook, flipflop, bosh, melliferous, bombinate, sonorous, resound, voluptuous, fragrant, vitriolic, gerrymander

I think that what pleases me about these words is primarily their "music." In some cases the meaning is already suggested by the way the word sounds; in others it is not, but even so

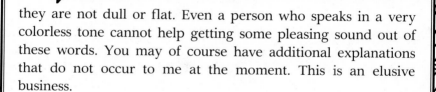

they are not dull or flat. Even a person who speaks in a very colorless tone cannot help getting some pleasing sound out of these words. You may of course have additional explanations that do not occur to me at the moment. This is an elusive business.

Albert Ellis
(Clinical psychologist, author, educator)

Meshugge—crazy, mixed up, addled. I love this word because it aptly describes practically all of my psychotherapy clients, because most of them nicely accept this description, and because they particularly accept it as being highly descriptive of their parents, close relatives, and intimate friends. Saying someone is crazy is often offensive; describing them as *meshugge* rarely is.

Alison Espach
(Author, *Adults*)

I don't know if it's my favorite word, but I used to say "like" all the time. It was the way kids spoke at that time. Like came in front of everything. I had to train myself out of saying it.

Willard Espy
(Author of a dozen books on language and language play)

My favorite word! You can't miss; I expect to find in it some of the most irresistible essays since Ivor Brown's. I doubt, though, whether I can be of much use, partly because of my utter lack of energy these days and partly because any word I may happen to utter or write at any instant is for that instant my favorite of them all, the best thing that ever happened—until the following word shoulders it aside. Words are *all* my favorites, like women.

If you had said the most beautiful word, or the ugliest word, the job would have been a little simpler. A few years ago I made an arbitrary choice of the ten most beautiful words in

English for *The Book of Lists,* and they have recently asked me to provide them with the ten ugliest for their next edition. That will be harder. As far as I can see, people are not appalled by gutturals or fricatives or spirants, but by meanings; the only word with an ugly meaning that I will agree is beautiful is "diarrhea."

But though I cannot provide you with my favorite word, I can indeed mention the one that is preoccupying me at the moment—one I consider to be worth your prayerful consideration. It is "velleity" (L. *velie,* to wish). Velleity is the lowest degree of desire, the slightest of wishes, the faintest of hopes. It is an inclination so near to none that it will never be acted on; and any disappointment at not acquiring the object so inertly desired will be as faint as the desire was. The lotus eaters had more get up and go to them than velleitists have. At any moment they may not bother to take the next breath, and it will take an autopsist a long time to decide whether they are alive or dead. "Velleity" is one of the saddest words in the world.

Gloria Estefan
(Singer)

My three favorite words are "houndation," "weirdness," and "plethora."

Dame Edna Everage
(aka Barry Humphries)

Dame Edna's favorite word is "spooky."

Douglas Fairbanks, Jr.
(Actor)

I have read your request for "my favorite words" and would be delighted to give you a few of mine. I have listed them in no particular order and chosen them because of their meanings, sounds, and uses.

rush	chases	shoulder
ruffle	five	shun
round	gesture	thorn
royal	heaven	thee
shame	languid	thou
sure	lazy	thine
surely	mentor	vine
velvet	money	wine
violin	noun	wisdom
wisteria	owl	yes
Aswan Dam	pheasant	zeal
Ashes	query	zealous
sugar	hush	

Jules Feiffer

(Pulitzer Prize-winning cartoonist; screenwriter;
playwright; author, *Backing into Forward*)

word of wisdom :

DUCK !

Bruce Feirstein

(Author, screenwriter, *Real Men Don't Eat Quiche*;
From Russia With Love video game)

Writers traffic in words.

Admittedly, there are those who would argue that our real currency is ideas. But words—and the ability to strike them together into cogent sentences and paragraphs—words are what separate us from the guys who came up with SaladShooters, Keogh plans, bungee jumping, and steel-cage fight-to-the death tag-team professional wrestling matches.

The words I like best are onomatopes or onomatopoetic: words that sound like what they describe. "Thunder." "Lightning." "Earthquake," "mud slide," "sonic boom." (On the other hand, maybe I'm just a sucker for the Great Creator's special effects.) I like "oleaginous" (as in "another oleaginous investment banker"), because it sounds slick; the word "obligatory" (it rolls off the tongue like a Mosler safe), plus "titanic" and "tectonic plates." (I'm not sure why, but to my ears, they just sound massive.) I also admire "lube job" (possibly because it sounds vaguely obscene) and "flotilla." Especially "flotilla." For me, it evokes tall ships, billowing sails, and an armada cutting through the mist at dawn. (Of all the sentences I've written, I think my favorite is "A flotilla of sleepy-eyed limousines cruised up Madison Avenue.")

Winston Churchill once said that "old words are best, and short words are best of all."

My single favorite word meets both these criteria. I enjoy hearing it most in response to the following questions. "Will you publish the book?"

"Will it be on the best-seller list?"

"Will it make a million dollars?"

And that word, of course, is:

"Yes."

Joseph Finder
(Best-selling author; *Paranoia*; *Company Man*; *Killer Instinct*; and *Buried Secrets*)

Henry James may have liked "cellar door," but if we're talking beautiful words no matter what they mean, what about *melanoma*? Like a susurrant wave (ooh) lapping against the shore of your mouth. Medicine gives us a treasure trove of euphony, including my favorite, *Hemoglobinopathy*. Just bounces back and forth between lips and palate, and really fun to say. Not fun to have, though. So if we rule out terrible diseases or unpleasant meanings, I'd nominate two slate of candidates. Sexiest: *salacious* and *lubricious*. Most beautiful: *mellifluous*, *sinuous*, and *melody*. But I wouldn't exactly kick *synesthesia* (or her English cousin, *synaesthesia*) out of bed either.

Gary Fisketjon
(Vice president, editor-at-large, Alfred A. Knopf, Inc.)
"Arete" (from the Greek).

Milos Forman
(Academy Award-winning film director)

When I came to America for the first time, all English words sounded to my ear equally nonsensical, but one sounded more nonsensical than the others, and that is probably why I developed a strange fondness for it and started to use it quite often.

This word not only expressed with great accuracy the level of my English, but with the same accuracy also described the expressions on the faces of my listeners: "discombobulated."

Dick Francis
(Edgar Award-winning author, *Forfeit*; *Whip Hand*;
Come to Grief; *Longshot*; *Crossfire*)

My favorite word is "Loyalty." As a jockey one should be loyal to one's owner and one's trainer, and to the public who might have backed your mount.

In addition, as an author one should be loyal to one's readers. One shouldn't incorporate plots or subplots into one's stories just to lead readers up the garden path and which have nothing whatsoever to do with the story.

Richard Frances
(Clinical professor of Psychiatry, New York University
Medical School; general editor, *A Clinical Textbook
of Addictive Disorders*)

I nostalgically love the words "hermeneutics" and "vicissitudes." Hermeneutics is the science of interpretation, which psychoanalysts and psychiatrists like to take as their special purview. Vicissitudes are the changes that occur in one's narcissism in relation to self and others that keep life interesting. In the heyday of psychoanalysis, there was little question that interpretation was a science and little question about who knew best how to interpret. The vicissitudes of narcissism were on every psychiatrist's lips at meetings, though the word never would be used with patients. In fact, in those days we didn't talk that much with patients—we listened—and when we did speak, we avoided highfalutin jargon. In the era of Jane Brody, the consuming public has grown expert, there is less need for biblical scholars to interpret the Bible, and increasingly patients look askance at our noble search for meaning. As for the vicissitudes of our professional self-regard, these are rough times for psychiatrists, who may not have all the answers but who strive for better tools to help patients. Nowadays, Hermes, the caduceus-carrying god who brought scientific messages in the old days only to those with white hair and advanced

training, brings hermeneutics to the mass culture; and alas, it is probably better that way.

Bruce Jay Friedman
(Author, humorist, *Stern*; *Scuba Duba*; *The Slightly Older Man*; *Lucky Bruce*)

"Wonder" is my favorite word, nosing out "residual." I'm always wondering about things, my characters are, too. It occurs to me, as I write this that the hero, such as he is, in my play *Scuba Duba* is named Harold Wonder. I no longer wonder why.

Lewis Burke Frumkes
(Author, *How to Raise Your I.Q. by Eating Gifted Children*; *Metapunctuation*)

My favorite words have changed over the years. When I was a youngster of ten or twelve, for example, reading a lot of romantic novels about knights in shining armor and princesses and things, I was fascinated by the word "gadzooks," which seemed to be the exclamation of choice to evoke in the presence of a dragon, say, or a hydra-headed monster that was blocking your way. I, however, adapted it to fit just about every situation whether it was appropriate or not, "Gadzooks, if it isn't Peter Green," I would say, or "Gadzooks, it's a peanut butter sandwich again today."

Sensational as "gadzooks" was at the time, people grew tired of hearing it two or three hundred times a day, and begged me to abandon it for more sophisticated locutions. So I moved on to "Barsoom," and "Barsoomian," which were the words John Carter of Mars, my hero, discovered were the correct Martian words to describe that faraway planet and its inhabitants. It is amazing how Barsoomian a grapefruit can look when you really think about it, or an ugly friend, or a dog for that matter. To this day my brother calls me Woola in an affectionate way, the name of a Barsoomian dog. (See *Roy Frumkes*.)

When I began to write professionally some years later, the words "kumquat" and "eggplant" seemed to surface more often in my writing than other words, which was curious (another favorite word) and may have had more to do with the shape of the objects, ovoid, than with their sounds ... I'm an egg man.

In any event, I am attracted as well to words such as seductive, cute, beguiling, ineluctable, dark, fabled, littoral, apodictic, *mariposa, Schmetterling,* moor, and redolent, for some reason, and to magical words such as djinn, mage, fey, oneiric, and enchantment. I might also include "taflespitz," a word that sends chills up and down my spine ... It's either a wonderful Viennese boiled beef dish frequently enhanced by horseradish sauce ... or a gorgeous German dominatrix. Take your pick.

I frequently lace my discourse with words such as lace, engaging, alluring, dragoon, eloquent, and droll, but see no apparent reason for this other than euphony and, I suppose, the images these words conjure up. While I do love many words in and of themselves for a host of aesthetic reasons, and wonder about other people's favorite words and why they love them (which is the *raison d'être* for this book), ultimately it is the way one arranges favorite words, juggles them in sequence and context, that determines the rhetorical direction and effectiveness of one's thought and ideas.

Melvin B. Frumkes
(Matrimonial lawyer)

I am delinquent and dilatory, which obviously leads to dangerous defalcations.

Hopefully, you will still be able to use the following pearls and gems of wisdom, notwithstanding that which is pronounced belies its meaning and intent.

Yup! My words are "Do it now."

I have those words emblazoned on my desks both in the office and at home, and I *try,* in most cases (except this), to adhere to it.

"Do it now." My children, now all adults, can hear those words in their sleep.

My clients are warned to adhere.

Opposing counsel quake with the thought of Motions for Enforcement and/or Contempt if the thundering admonition of "Do it now" is not adhered to.

My junior associates, paralegals, clerks, and secretaries all know the rules and rarely dare to stray from the mandatory fiat.

The words "Do it now" have served me well, enabling me to meet all kinds of deadlines (that is, all those on which I am able to get an extension), which usually accomplishes wonderful results in the acrimonious litigation in which I am involved.

Roy Frumkes

(Filmmaker/screenwriter, *The Substitute*; *The Sweet Life*; professor at the School of Visual Arts)

I asked the book's author if nicknames counted, and he decided they did. Which is good, because although I love sensual, mellifluous words like " mellifluous," I always feel a little pretentious using them, which skims the cream off them (as in Brown Cow yogurt), and I like cream with my words.

I've had only a few close friends and family members during my life, and their nicknames are precious to me. When I was young, for instance, my father, for some unknown reason called me "Yussel." When I hit my early teens, I started calling *him* "Yussel." I must have done it religiously, or with some extraordinary sense of conviction, because it stuck. Eventually people who scarcely knew my father were calling him Yussel. By the time I reached my twenties, I rarely even associated myself with its inspiration. On the few occasions when his real name—Harry—would be mentioned, it sounded all wrong. He didn't look like a Harry. He looked like a Yussel. Then I learned that Harry had been a nickname given him by his fifth-grade teacher. His real name was William.

My closest friend for twenty-five years was Robert Janes Winston. When I met him in the eighth grade, he had already been dubbed "Winnie" by his playmates. I picked up the gauntlet. Over the years we did some screenwriting together, and one idea—*The Comeback Trail*—ended up being directed by a filmmaker named Harry Hurwitz. One day Harry asked me why I called Winnie by that name. I tried to explain. He came down on me pretty hard about using nicknames, insisting the practice was childish, etc. Later, a friend of his named Martin Smith visited the office, and I heard Harry calling him "Smitty." What's more, he spotted me hearing him calling him Smitty, looked as if he'd been caught doing something wrong and childish, and from then on always addressed his friend—at least in front of me—as Martin. I just went right on calling Winnie "Winnie."

As to my older brother, the renowned humorist who so kindly invited me to contribute to this book, the moniker he's had to live with for many years is "Woola," from *A Princess of Mars* by Edgar Rice Burroughs, Woola being a six-legged Martian dog of great size, ferocious demeanor, and devoted heart. None of these attributes had anything to do with why my brother ended up saddled with the name. Well, maybe the great size ... (just kidding, Woola!). I think if it evolved from anything, it was a failed anagram. "Woola" rearranged should spell "Lewis." It doesn't, but the good intentions are there.

Actually, there is one attribute of the Martian Woola that does, coincidentally, fit my brother, and that is the good heart. Surely this must be true, considering all the "Woola"s he's had to endure, many of them even in public.

Cristina Garcia
(Author, *Dreaming in Cuban*; *Monkey Hunting*; *A Handbook to Luck*)

"Piglet"—because I love diminutives and English, unlike Spanish, is so lacking in them.

"Hamlet"—ditto and because we Cubans take our roast pork seriously.

Howard Gardner
(Harvard educational psychologist and author who introduced and popularized the notion of "multiple intelligences")

It turns out that I care the most about little words and, most especially, about that delightful particle "yet." Most of my writing harbors on the academic, and so I am usually arguing in favor of, or against, some point of view. To begin, I like to set up a tenable counterargument or strawperson, one that has at least surface plausibility. At that point, "yet" enters the picture, along with its cousins "however"; but in contrast, or that lovely sentence opener: "And yet."

In addition to its compact size, its decisive sound (so reminiscent of the Russian *nyet),* and its hint of optimism, "yet" also documents how much work can be accomplished by a simple concatenation of three letters. It is the family of "yet"— but, and, indeed, moreover, therefore, notwithstanding—and their numerous relatives that permit us to continue arguments, to signal readers about where we have been, where we are going, and how one should feel about each point along the voyage. They supply needed lights in a sea of dark prose.

Most of my fights with copy editors occur around these little words. Some copy editors don't like them at all; some do not want to use them to signal a change of direction; some have their favorite conjunctions and interjections, which happen not to coincide with mine. If I ever challenge a copy editor to a duel, it will probably be prompted by a dropped "yet" or a mangled "in the event."

I lay no claim to be the first to signal the power of these little words. After all, Paul Pierre Broca identified an entire variety of aphasia that features the deletion of these words; Shakespeare's most famous soliloquy begins with six little words, five of them consisting of only two letters each; and I understand that an entire doctoral dissertation has been written on the meaning of the formidable German particle *doch*. And yet, if I am not among the first, I hope that I may be counted among the most faithful advocates of "yet."

William H. Gass

(American Book Award–winning author,
The Tunnel; *Finding a Form*)

There's a philosopher whom I admire very much, Gaston Bachellard, who wrote a wonderful book early in his career on the philosophy of science called *The Philosophy of Know*. In that book he develops what he calls the obstacle concept, and he has a little test whereby you look into yourself to find your talismanic word. It's your favorite and probably your greatest enemy. And when I started to investigate this when I was teaching his book, I found out quickly mine was "form."

I'm basically a romantic writer and so for many, many years—including work in philosophy, which was so rigorously analytic—I hunted for the process of taming this wild impulse and so on, and bringing it into a very complex formal interconnection. And of course my theory about the nature of art is basically a formalist theory, but behind it is this Nietzchean who tries to be ridden by Wittgenstein.

Murray Gell-Mann

(Nobel Prize in physics, 1969; author, *The Quark and the Jaguar*)
"Quark." See *Calvin and Hobbes*, 1993.

Paolo Giordano
(Award-winning author, *The Solitude of Prime Numbers*)

"Empathy" is my favorite word because it drives me until I can get to where I want to go. I also use the words of body parts a lot in writing a first draft; face, hands, etc. "Deep" is another of the words I like.

Penn Gillette
(Entertainer, magician, Penn & Teller)

"Ruckus" is my favorite word.

Nikki Giovanni
(Poet, playwright, *Cypress, Sassafras & Indigo*; *For Colored Girls*)

If by "favorite" we mean the word we most use, then mine clearly is "illogical." There is, of course, no reason to think human beings should be logical, but the optimist in me insists, thereby forcing me to conclude: illogical when the unacceptable intrudes. On the other hand, my happiest word is "moile," which is really not a word but a feeling. When I am happy, I feel like a happy moile. A moile looks like a who with a Santa Claus laugh. Good things come from moiles. I wrote a poem about it.

Sheldon Glashow
(Mellon Professor of the Sciences, Harvard University; Nobel Prize winner, physics)

Professionally, "charm" is my beloved because I used it to characterize the fourth quark flavor long before it was found. It is indeed a device to ward off evil, if by "evil" is meant a conflict between experiment and theory.

"Radii" and "skiing" both have double *i*'s, but only "hajji" does it for *i*. No English word competes with German *Schneeeule*, since "headmistress-ship" is hyphenated. "Indivisibility" has

more *i*'s than any other word I know except its plural, which has seven. Finally, can you find a word longer than "assesses" containing no string of three different letters?

Julia Glass

(National Book Award–winning author, *Three Junes*; *The Whole World Over*; *The Widower's Tale*)

Widdershins

As a child, I was a robust consumer of folklore from every conceivable culture. One of my favorite books was a volume of Joseph Jacobs' fairy tales, with commentary by W. H. Auden (though his name did not impress me then). The best and most haunting tale in the book was "Childe Rowland," which begins when three boys are playing ball with their sister on a church lawn and she vanishes into thin air. The brothers—who will, this being a fairy tale, set out on serial quests to rescue their sister—discover that she's been abducted by a sorcerer because she ran around the church widdershins: in the opposite direction to the sun (that is, counterclockwise).

From the moment I read that word aloud, I fell in love with it; I've used it more than once, though very selectively, in my fiction. To this day, it evokes mischief, superstition, and black magic, yet also the dire solemnity of saving a loved one from peril. (It also summons up a grisly illustration from the book: the youngest brother, the ultimate hero, in the necessary act of beheading an innocent horseherd.) During an extremely painful period of loss and grief in my midthirties, I remember thinking that it felt as if my life had gone widdershins. Just now, pulling that book off a shelf and paging through it for the first time in a few years, I dipped into Auden's charming afterword and learned that a Scottish synonym for widdershins is *wrang-gaites*—and that the opposite of widdershins is *deiseal*. How many rich, delicious words the world contains, and how fortunate I am to be in the business of using them!

Harrison J. Goldin

(Former comptroller, City of New York)

I love words, all words, the very idea of words—their precision, their color, their subtlety, their sound. But I have special associations with some that distinguish them from all the others and evoke a particular thought or recollection.

Most of all there is "hereon," not for its euphony or clarity or romance, but because it reminds me of an occasion. Years ago, when I was much younger and before our children were born, on a beautiful summer Sunday afternoon, my wife, Diana, and I would sometimes take a leisurely spin on our motorcycle along country roads near our home in Dutchess County. The fides were exhilarating—the warm breeze at our faces, she holding on to me tight, the beautiful scenery, the joy of intimacy between us and nature. One such day, as the miles sped by, I turned my head to her slightly and, as she leaned in to listen, said, "Have you ever heard of this guy Here-e-on? He must be the biggest landowner in the Hudson Valley!" Sure enough, on every "posted" sign we passed (the ones that warn trespassers to keep off private property) was prominently displayed (on nearly every other tree) the name of the apparent proprietor, always in big black letters, "Hereon." I racked my brain; we conferred. We knew that Roosevelts, Vanderbilts, Morgenthaus, even lesser lights of our acquaintance were large landowners in the area. But a Mr. "Hereon?" Perhaps a mysterious Wall Street tycoon, or a South American. Pronouncing it "Here-e-on," as we did, made it seem vaguely Scottish or even Celtish. Suddenly, we both slapped our foreheads at the same time, feeling simultaneously foolish. I stopped the motorcycle and read aloud. "No trespassing," the sign said in small letters, "HEREON," in thick, black bold ones. The secret tycoon was unmasked, the mystery solved.

From that day to this, whenever I meander on country lanes and see posted land, I remember that lovely day, how perplexed I had been and how silly I felt. Mr. Here-e-on indeed!

AI Goldstein

(Founder/Publisher, *Screw* magazine)

"Chocolate" and/or "Bangkok."

Rebecca Goldstein

(Author, *The Mind-Body Problem*; *Mazel*;
36 Arguments for the Existence of God)

Many of the words that I love, I love for their origins: *mesmerize* because it sounds like what it means, even though it exists only through the happy accident of Franz Mesmer's having experimented with animal magnetism. *Ecstasy* also pleases me for its source, for the lovely metaphysics that unfolds from its etymology: the self's standing beside itself. These are words that appeal to me for more or less respectable (i.e., scholarly) reasons. My more idiosyncratic logophiliac choices (for which there is no doubt some Freudian explanation of which I have no desire to know) are words that describe the motions of water: *splash* lifts my spirit, and *plash*, because it's even more particular—a little splash—you can hear it—takes me over the top. *Trickle, dripple, billow, eddy.* Even so common an item as *spill*, suggestive of things gone awry, of loss of control and uncontainment; but yet, because it is of watery mishaps that it speaks, it pleases me.

Adam Gopnik

(*New Yorker* writer; author, *Paris to the Moon*;
Angels and Ages)

Favorite words. What a good question, Lewis! "Consequences," the word. I remember years ago I was studying art history and I had all the bad habits of an academic writer, a pedantic writer—I would argue everything out—and then sitting alone one day in a room writing I discovered the enormous power of "and" and "then." That if you string statements and observations together with simple connectives like "and" and "then," which is a time connective, the narrative could then begin. I discovered

you could write with real authority—which was a revelation—if you wrote with "ands" and "thens" instead of "buts" and "therefores." Now when I teach creative writing, I try to instruct my students to write with "ands" and "thens" rather than "buts" and "therefores." In fact, if I had two words I could inscribe as my own epitaph it would be, "And then."

Al Gore
(Former Vice President of the United States; Nobel laureate)

One of my favorite words is *interstitial*, but a word that I like even more and use quite often is the mathematical term *asymptotic*.

Edward Gorey
(Cartoonist, creator/illustrator; author, *Amphigorey*; *The Curious Sofa*; *The Haunted Tea-Cosy*)

My favorite word is "silence"; it would be perverse to go on.

Virginia Graham
(Actress, television personality)

I have always been a devotee of outrageous and explicit hyperbole, and an adjective has a release from too many social restraints.

So, as we get more mature (I hate the word "older"), I have substituted such words as:

"I find this 'exceedingly inappropriate'"; "inappropriate" might be used instead of "How could you invite three former wives to your party?"

"I think you looked so much better before your face adjustment."

"Some people lose all their looks when they get fat."

All may be true, but inappropriate.

Alan "Ace" Greenberg
(Former CEO, Bear Stearns & Co.)

"Omphaloskepsis."

Dan Greenburg
(Author, *How to Be a Jewish Mother*; *Exes*)

"Basically": Since I was a senior in college, whenever I've wished to parody the fatuous, the pretentious, or the pedantic, I have interjected the word "basically" into almost every phrase. Needless to say, I also interject the word "basically" whenever I'm being fatuous, pretentious, or pedantic myself.

"Peppy": When Carl Reiner and Mel Brooks first came out with the *2,000 Year Old Man* record albums, my buddies and I listened to them so often, we soon had the routines committed to memory. Brooks' use of the word "peppy" insinuated itself into my speech and into my writing, where it remained for many years.

"Guy": I have always liked the informality of the word "guy." and tend to use it a bit more than I should.

Basically, I guess I'm just a peppy guy.

A. R. Gurney
(Playwright; novelist; *Love Letters*; *The Cocktail Hour*; and *The Dining Room*)

I don't really have a favorite word (I like them all) but Gil Parker, my former agent, thinks I have several favorite expressions such as "hunker down" and "review the bidding."

Mark Hamill
(Actor, Luke Skywalker in *Star Wars*)

One word that made a lasting impression on me is one I've never heard in everyday conversation. It was in a wonderful movie I saw with my family when I was perhaps eight or nine years old and seemed to contain a sense of magic and wonder that makes me smile to this very day.

The word? "Pixilated."

I have been dividing people into and out of this specific category ever since.

And yes—I am. Are you?

Helen Handley
(Poet, anthologist)

Words combined—phrases, sentences, paragraphs, and pages— give me such a boost! But there's the isolated word "also," which, like unaccompanied music, has its own surprises of tone and resonance. My favorite word is "serendipity"; it sounds springy, full of good luck, whoopee! Thanks to Horace Walpole, who gave us serendipity: happy accidents and unexpected discoveries; looking for one thing, we find another, which is what we really wanted all along. I also like "smooth," "enshrine," and "bouquet." "Words exhale temperament," said the late Howard Moss. So there's something of mine.

Donna Hanover
(Former First Lady of the City of New York and author, *My Boyfriend's Back*)

My favorite word is "fluxxmoxed." Not a word at all, you say? Let me explain. When I was writing the book *My Boyfriend's Back,* about couples who reunite later in life, as I did with my high school sweetheart, Ed Oster, he was very patient. In spite of my sixteen-hour days at the computer, lack of makeup, and diet of popcorn and M&M's, he stepped up as a great husband,

devoting extra time to his law practice and to being the best imaginable proofreader for the book. When he got to the sentence that I had written late one bleary-eyed night, "... some mothers and fathers are fluxxmoxed by their children's choice in a love interest," he laughed out loud. Yes, we agreed with the editors to change it to "flummoxed." But the typo version just has more punch. So in our everyday language, when seeking a synonym for bewildered, puzzled, perplexed, flustered, or baffled, we always turn to our invented word as in "When we think back on our early romance, we are fluxxmoxed that we could ever have broken up!"

Josephine Hart
(Author, playwright, *Damage*; *Sin*; *Oblivion*)

For some reason or other the actual word "onomatopoeia" is a favorite; I love saying it. The line that I love and which resonates endlessly with me is, "Footfalls echo in the memory down the passage which we did not take towards the door—we never opened into the rose-garden." I repeat that line by Elliot over and over in my mind because it's an astonishing juxtaposition of concepts within a great poetic gift. To have footfalls echo in your memory down a passage that you never took ... I mean really, language doesn't get any better than that, does it? It's brilliant!

Don Hauptman
(Author, *Cruel and Unusual Puns*; *Acronymania*)

One of my favorite words is "festoon."

The proposal for my first book *Cruel and Unusual Puns* contained this sentence: "As a wicked parody of the excesses of academic journalese, I intend to festoon the Introduction with pseudoscholarly footnotes and deconstructionist analysis."

Every time the word came up in discussions with my agent, we broke into laughter, chuckles, and guffaws. And why not?

Certainly, "festoon" has an amusing sound, suggesting "festive" (to which it is related) and such "fun" words as "balloon," "bassoon," "buffoon," and "cartoon."

As things turned out, the particular festooning I had envisioned did not occur. But *Cruel* was a success, launching my second writing career, as an author of books on language and wordplay. Were I superstitious, I might have convinced myself that the word served as a good luck charm. "Festoon" derives, via French, from the Italian *festone,* literally a decoration for a feast *(festa)*. Its original meaning (a noun) is "a string or garland, as of leaves or flowers, suspended in a loop or curve between two points" *(American Heritage Dictionary,* third edition). "Festoon" subsequently came to mean a decorative reproduction of such a device, as, for example, an ornament in painting, sculpture, or architecture. The sense was then extended to other curved or scalloped shapes, such as an arrangement of fabric.

After checking a few dictionaries for this assignment, I concluded that my use of the word in the book proposal was more liberal than literal. But as a verb, in current parlance, I suspect that one can metaphorically festoon just about anything, simply by placing generous quantities of an item on or in it.

So don't just sit there. Go out and festoon something today!

Naura Hayden

(Author, *How to Satisfy a Woman Every Single Time*; *Astrological Love*)

I love funny words. "Tumleys" is possibly my favorite word, or maybe "duckum" or "derangel." These are my made-up words for the love of my life. Because he has a *great* sense of humor and we laugh a *lot,* particularly at silly things, I sometimes say "Tumleys is my derangel (and you *are* deranged!)", and that leads to some *really* silly stuff from him (he's much funnier than I, and you now may be thinking, well, *that* wouldn't be too difficult), but after rereading this, I think my *all-time* favorite word would be "goodness."

Maida Heatter
(Cookbook writer)

My favorite word is "chocolate." It's the most delicious word I know. Some scientists may question this, but there are millions of chocolate lovers who will vouch for the fact that eating chocolate makes them feel sixteen years old and madly, head-over-heels in love. And there are those who claim that it will cure whatever ails you. The word—if I read it or write it or say it—tastes just great to me.

Florence Henderson
(Actress, *The Brady Bunch*; host, *The Florence Henderson Show*)

What a great idea! I have now become totally obsessed with words. Following are a few of my favorites:

"Misnomer," "misconception"—because people always get them confused.

"Humanity"—because I worry there isn't enough in the world right now.

"Energy"—because it represents a joy in living—a life force.

"Spirit"—it makes me think of grace and compassion and it gives one the faith that they cannot be defeated in life!

"Exacerbate"—it sounds like something you do alone in the bathroom!

I also like "communication," "dedication," and "consecration." By this time I think you know why.*

*Editor's note: Florence is referring to the United Cerebral Palsy Telethon, for which she and Dennis James have worked tirelessly and unselfishly for many years as performers and hosts.

Tony Hendra

(Humorist, author, *Going Too Far*; *Father Joe*; *Last Words*)

My favorite word is *schmuck.*

When I came to New York in 1964, *schmuck* was the first American word I heard that made me laugh out loud. Even before I knew its literal meaning, I loved this word. And since the only people I knew back then were Jewish, I heard it a lot.

It's not just as a put-down. It evokes the warmth and friendliness of those who helped me come to America, who fed me, set me up, and showered me with presents, who bounced me around from one noisy, funny family to another, showed me the ropes in the city of my dreams, taught me to be a New Yorker, like them an easy touch under a hard-boiled exterior, and most important when to yell, drawl, snap, mutter, or simply sigh, "You *schmuck*!"

As a put-down, though, it's perfection. Unlike its hard-edged fricative and plosive Anglo-Saxon cousins, "schmuck" has a gentler, resigned quality to it. "Sure," it seems to be saying, "you exhibit a massive resemblance to the male sexual organ, but at least you're not a *putz.* "

Bob Hope

(Comic, actor, national treasure)

My favorite word of all time is "laughter," and when I am asked why, I reply, why not?

A. E. Hotchner

(Author, *Hemingway and His World*; *King of the Hill: A Memoir*; cofounder, Newman's Own)

I am increasingly partial to the word "philanthropy." By Webster's definition: "A desire to help mankind as indicated by acts of charity, service, gifts, etc.; love of mankind." It is a word that encompasses an act as simple as taking a bundle of clothes to the Goodwill or as complex as donating ten million to a university.

Hemingway once said, speaking of his own philosophy, that "you don't own anything until you give it away." "Philanthropy" is a word that defines that act: reading for the blind; devoting hours to Literacy Volunteers; giving blood; donating a sum to the local hospital, your alma mater, AIDS research, whatever cause concerns you. For the past twelve years, Paul Newman and I have had the good fortune of running a prospering good company that generates millions of dollars of profit every year, every penny of which we give away at year's end to a wide variety of needy causes, ranging from cancer research to field schools for the children of migrant workers. We are blessed with this largesse of philanthropy, and I never tire of hearing the word or seeing it on the printed page.

Arianna Huffington
(Cofounder, *The Huffington Post*)

"Trust"; trust in life; trust in God; trust that the Universe is a friendly place; trust that, incredible though it may sound, "not a sparrow falls without His knowing"; trust that there is meaning in our pain and purpose to our lives; trust that we shall meet again; trust that life is a mystery to be lived, not a riddle to be solved—both unutterably sacred *and* the old banana-skin joke on a cosmic scale.

Derek Humphry
(Founder, the Hemlock Society; author, *Jean's Way*; *Final Exit*)

Because most of my life has been devoted to writing and campaigning about civil liberties, my two favorite words are "choice" and "option." Nothing is dearer to me than the right to choose—freedom to read and write, freedom of thought, freedom of religion and from other people's religions, abortion or adoption, life or death (although we don't have any choice about the finality of death, we can sometimes speed it or slow it). If one takes the long view of how Western society is developing, as the traditional shackles on individual behavior evaporate, obviously words like "choice" and "option" will achieve greater usage and significance.

Evan Hunter

(Author, *The Blackboard Jungle*; aka Ed McBain, author of more than eighty crime novels, including *Mary, Mary*)

I've pondered and repondered your question, and for the life of me I cannot think of a favorite word. My favorite color is blue. Does that help?

Susan Isaacs

(Author, *Compromising Positions*; *After All These Years*; *As Husbands Go*)

I'm fickle. There is no one word to which I've remained faithful. Instead, I have relationships that last from a few weeks to a year or two, until I get bored and move on. I've gone from "terrific" to "dandy" and am currently flirting with "swell." I've forsaken "fungible" and "quasi-" and dropped "subanthropoidal" like a hot potato.

Pico Iyer

(Essayist, *Time* magazine; author, *Falling off the Map*; *The Open Road*)

"Languorous." I like the ease, the recline, the slowness that amounts to sensuousness in this word; I like its sense of recumbency, the way it sprawls out like a hammock between the trees, and confounds somehow the casual speller (with its odd—almost unique—conjunction of *uo* and *ou*). I like its liquidity, its looseness, its closeness to all the other lovely *l* words that roll sleepily off the tongue—such as "leisure" and "lulling" and lithe." "Languorous" is very much a romance word, a romantic word, a word that belongs in the sun. It has an ugly brother, of course, but "languid" has something clipped about it, sullen

and even pouting; "languorous," by contrast, is outstretched and openhearted. Its Latin cousins, born of the same roots, are "relax" and "release" and "relish," and its very heart—that uncanny "uorou"—sounds like a South Sea love song.

Nothing shocking, you notice, ever happens languorously; nobody ever shouts or agitates languorously. "Languorous" describes the purl of the sea, or the breeze between the palms; it belongs to those enchanted souls who live beyond care or inhibition. Life's pleasures are almost always "languorous," its nightmares almost never.

So it is that the places we dream of are "languorous places," and they call to us like trade winds. "Languorous" involves a sloughing off of time and space, a slipping off of rules, a shedding of hard edges. "Languorous" ushers us, in fact, into a world of sighs.

Rona Jaffe

(Author, *The Best of Everything*; *Class Reunion*)

In my first novel I was partial to the word "whispered," as used in dialogue when one of my girls was asking a question the answer to which she dreaded, such as: "Do you mean you don't love me anymore?" "Whispered" was a humble and frightened word. As I grew older and stronger and my "girls" became women, they began to "say" and "ask." Not that they don't sometimes still dread the answer! I save whispering for a more cheerful context, but use it rarely because it's quite strong. I still think it's a nice word, though, because it sounds like what it does.

Dennis James
(Television personality; host, United Cerebral Palsy Telethon)

My life has been full of "skidsomycetees" (little things with no payoff). I am always pressured by my wife with "forcenahobbs" (do this ... do that). It's a "framus" (pain). Those are three of my words: "skidsomycetees," "forcenahobbs," and "framus."

Morton Janklow
(Literary agent, Janklow & Nesbit Associates)

My two favorite words are "windowsill" and "turquoise." I have no particular psychological association with these words—I just love the sound of them.

Tama Janowitz
(Author, *Slaves of New York*; *They Is Us*)

I have always liked the words "oolitic limestone." Dry, friable, slightly sour, and crumbly on the tongue—something about the name of this rock reflects what it is exactly. There are also many other kinds of igneous, metamorphic, and sedimentary rock that I have always thought had appealing names: gypsum, feldspar, slate, schist, mica, jasper, and agate are just a few.

Gish Jen
(Author, *Who's Irish*; *The Love Wife*;
Mona In The Promised Land; *World And Town.*)

My favorite word is "resonant."

Franklyn G. Jenifer
(President emeritus of the University of Texas at Dallas)

One word that I tend to use frequently in both speaking and writing is "bold." There is something about the very boldness of the word that appeals to me (i.e., it sounds so much like what it means). It also has a nice sound to it, with that full, round *o*.

Often I use the word in the context of what higher education and other leaders must do to address the problems that confront them (i.e., they must be bold). In a recent speech I gave at a meeting of the Middle States Association of Colleges and Schools, for instance, I used the word on several occasions ("higher educational leaders who dare to be bold"; "bold research"; "bold initiatives of productivity"; "we must be bold enough to say to the old guard ...").

To give another example: Near the end of my opinion piece about the value and validity of predominantly black colleges, published in the October 16, 1991, issue of *The Chronicle of Higher Education,* I wrote:

> Moreover, we must be bold enough to assert—proudly and loudly—that some higher education institutions are predominantly black for compelling historical and sociological reasons, and that, because of those compelling reasons, they should stay that way now and for some time to come.

Somehow I don't think any other word would have done justice to such a bold statement as, yes, "bold."

Richard Jenrette
(Former CEO, Donaldson, Lufkin & Jenrette, The Equitable)

I loved your book. It is delicious (that was Jacqueline Onassis's favorite word ... everything was "delicious".)

I like the word *perceived* for some reason. It implies a mystical power to see things not clear to others. If you "perceive" something to be true, no one can argue. If you say something is true, you'll get an argument.

Richard Johnson
(Editor, *The Daily*)

I love the word *bogus*. It's better than *phony*, or *fake*, or *faux*. It's even better than *claptrap*, *poppycock*, and *horsefeathers*.

Erica Jong
(Poet, author, *Fear of Flying*; *The Devil at Large*; *Fear of Fifty*; *Sappho's Leap*)

Breath, Death, Pillicocks, and Picklocks

In my teens and twenties, in love with language, I pored over dictionaries and thesauri and made lists of words like: maenad, mead, pelisse, parquetry, viridian, verdancy, rubescence ... Then I devised poems in which I could use them. "The rubescence of the Rubens nudes," I said ruddily in one line. "Green virility" shimmered elsewhere on the page. "Parquetries of mellow wood" glowingly seduced the reader's ear and eye. In other poems maenads went mad in meadows, no doubt from drinking too much mead, and sprites wore pink pelisses (perhaps made of flamingo feathers). How reassured I was to find my practice validated by W. H. Auden in *The Dyers's Hand:* "A poet has to woo, not only his own Muse, but also Dame Philology and, for the beginner, the latter is more important." Aha—when a young poet loves words above content—it's a good sign.

Words meant so much to me for so long that I was even moved to write a whole novel in eighteenth-century English, *Fanny Hackabout Jones.* There I could indulge my word-listings to my heart's content and still keep the plot moving. "Pillicock," "picklock," "love-dart" were some of the terms my heroine used for the masculine member when she was reduced to whoring in a London brothel circa 1728. Surely some of my delight in writing this novel came from the eighteenth-century language of love itself, which was at once more poetic and blunter than our debased cant for the art of love.

But now, in the middle of my life, I am no longer in love with fancy words. As I feel time's wings beating at my back, I write headlong, *try*ing to use words to get *beyond* words. Perhaps flesh cannot stay, but surely, breath can.

"Breath" is my favorite word today. It is like "flesh," but more ethereal. Like "breast," but even warmer and moister. Like love, it makes us rise. It begins with lips together, but it ends with lips open and the tongue touching the palate's arch. All of life is in this word. And it rhymes with nothing but "death." That should tell us something.

Michio Kaku
(Theoretical physicist, author, *Hyperspace*)

My favorite word is "falsifiable," which is the acid test of any true scientific theory. In fact, it captures the essence of science. As Nobel laureate Richard Feynman used to quip, "The mission of every physicist is to prove yourself wrong as quickly as possible." In other words, you're free to dream of any theory you want, under the strict admonition that you must try your best to poke holes in it. If the theory falls apart, then you have saved yourself a lot of time. If you can't find anything wrong with it, then perhaps you have discovered something important about the universe.

Religion, by its very nature, fails this simple test. Miracles, encounters with angels, exorcisms, feats of magic, etc. are not falsifiable. How do you place an angel in a laboratory? Miracles, by definition, only happen once in a lifetime, and hence are not reproducible, let alone falsifiable.

I try, with only limited success, to tell my mystical friends about this simple test. Reincarnation, ghosts, and channeling by 10,000- year-old-spirits are not falsifiable, and hence not scientific.

Bel Kaufman
(Author, *Up the Down Staircase*)

I offer you four:

The first that comes to mind is "no!" It's a powerful word, which I have begun to use only in my late years, when I realized that I was entitled to speak my mind, that I did not need to be loved or accepted by everyone, and that I had the wisdom to know what I wanted and what I did not want.

By contrast, the word "yes" was one I used when I was young, buying love and acceptance with my compliance. Of course, "no" may have deprived me of some positive offers in my life, and "yes" condemned me to acquiesce to the second-best, but on the whole, I am pleased at my present ability to make a choice.

A word that has always given me great pleasure both for its sound and its evocative quality is "onomatopoeia," and its adjective, "onomatopoetic." It makes me think of *buzzing* bees and *beeping* beeps, and it has a kind of elegance I like.

A fourth word is "cozy." It never fails to make me think of fireplaces and warm blankets and nestling someplace, curled up, snug and warm, with a book or an apple or both. The sound itself is a cozy one: the *o* round and friendly, the *z* easy on the tongue. It almost sings.

Gene Kelly
(Actor/dancer, *Singing in the Rain*)

Herewith are a few of my favorite words.

Like most words, I like to hear them said out loud. I like the sound of them better than seeing them in print.

My favorite: "plethora."
Some others: "blending"
       "siesta"
       "succubus."

Say them out loud ... they really sing!

Judith Kelman
(Author, *The House on the Hill*; *Someone's Watching*;
Summer of Storms)

My favorite word, no contest, is "serendipity." I like the feel and sound of it. I enjoy the lingual challenge, sort of an advanced Step Reebok workout for the tongue. Above all, I appreciate the value of serendipity: mining for unexpected positives in the cosmic pie throw that is life. As my mother often says, "Rich or poor, it's nice to have money," but that's for another book.

Serendipitously, when you remove the dip, you wind up with "serenity." I'll nominate that as my first runner-up. If, at any time during its reign, "serendipity" should prove unable to fulfill its duties, "serenity" will suit me fine.

Rose Kennedy
(Mother of President John F. Kennedy and
Senator Edward M. Kennedy)

At 102 years old and very frail, Mrs. Kennedy responded to my query through her deputy press secretary, Melody Miller, who said:

"Her favorite word is 'faith.' Considering all she has been through in her lifetime, I believe that this word is an understandable choice. Her faith has been the sustaining force in her life."

Florence King
(Author, *With Charity Towards None*)

I like words calculated to bring a blush to a feminist's cheek. I am a "spinster" because I have never married. I am "barren" because I have had the menopause, which is also why I no longer have "affairs": my "desire" is gone. I am not "single" because that can mean anything and usually does; I am not "sterile" because that describes males and I am female; I have never had "relationships" because they sound intolerably earnest, and I have never had a "sex drive" because it sounds as if it belongs in a graph instead of a bed. I believe in using one time-honored word, not two or three faddish buzzwords, that says exactly what I mean and that cannot possibly mean anything else. That way lies "precision"—perhaps my favorite word of all because I can hear the ball bearing rolling through it.

I also love "profanity." My mother was a muleskinner cusser in the great tradition of the U.S. Cavalry, capable of dazzling cascades and ingenious combinations that put today's unimaginative "obscenity" to shame. Her favorite epithet— "double asshole, shit sandwich, five-alarm turd sonofabitch"— sounds like a 100 mph fastball whizzing down the middle and thudding into the catcher's mitt. Abe Lincoln was right: all that I am or hope to be I owe to my angel mother.

Larry King
(Host, *Larry King Live*)

My favorite word is "why." I use it more than any other— professionally and otherwise. It begins a lot of my questions, and it can't be answered with one word. It's probably the best word in the universe. Think about it.

John Kluge
(Former chairman and president, Metromedia Company)

My favorite word is "yes."

Elizabeth Kostova
(Author, *The Historian*; *The Swan Thieves*)

"Lucubrations," the deep thoughts you have at three in the morning. I used it in *The Historian*, but couldn't find a way to work it into *The Swan Thieves*.

Paul Krassner

(Author, *Confessions of a Raving, Unconfined Nut; Who's to Say What's Obscene?*)

My favorite word is "change" because it is such a catalyst for subjective interpretation. To a clerk at the supermarket, it means "money." To an infant in a shopping cart, it means "diapers." To a shopper waiting on line, it means a new "self-help" program. And to me, it means the very process of "evolution." Also, that I might change my favorite word at any given moment.

Charles Krauthammer

(Essayist, columnist, *The Washington Post*;
commentator, Fox News Network)

It turns out that my favorite word is "preposterous." I wasn't aware of this until my wife pointed out the alarming regularity with which I use the word. It seems that I use it to describe most any opinion with which I disagree.

The word has two endearing qualities. First, it is rather gentle, in contrast to, say, "idiotic." Second, it expresses itself without need of translation. It is onomatopoeic. Pre-post-er-ous: Once all the syllables have rolled off the tongue, the word has done its work. What is an opinion thus calumnied to do but slink away in shame?

Bernard Kripke

(Computer scientist)

My favorite words have been stories, such as "bunkum," after the congressional representative who had been blathering on the floor of the House for the benefit of his constituents in Buncombe County, North Carolina. I once lived next door to a descendant of the Pennsylvania farmer who gave his name, "Haymaker," when he struck his neighbor dead with one punch. Another favorite is "hoist with one's own petard"—blown up by one's own explosive device (in French, a fart).

Amy Kugali
(Neuropublicist)

My favorite word has always been "lagniappe" because it's fun to say, and I like the way it's spelled, and I like its origin (southern Louisiana, where my kinfolk hail from), and of course because of its meaning—an unexpected gift, what a delightful thing!

Hedy Lamarr
(Actress, *Samson and Delilah*; *Ecstasy*)

"Empathy."

Wally Lamb
(Author, *She's Come Undone*; *I Know This to Be True*

Since I was a kid, for some reason, I've always loved the word "chandelier", the way it flows. I love the flow of language and for me, very often, there's a connection between language and the sound of running water. When I'm having a bad-writing day, one of the ways I can dislodge things is to hop in a car, or put on my sneakers and go to the sounds of running water, to a stream that's passing by, or a waterfall near where we live.

Another word that means a lot to me, both as a writer, and as a person, is "renovation." Ultimately that is the message of *I Know This to Be True*. If you do the work of renovating your life, of understanding who you are outside, or beyond the context of who you were the moment you arrived at the hospital—and go back into your past in terms of who your ancestors were—then renovation will point the way.

Ann Landers
(Syndicated columnist)

My favorite word is "chocolate." No question about it, I am addicted. It would be impossible for me to conquer this addiction because all my friends (and even some strangers) know that I am hooked. Barely a week goes by that I don't receive at least two boxes.

The word "chocolate" has a beautiful sound, and when I hear it, the juices start to flow, and I simply must find a piece of Fanny Farmer, Godiva, or Nestlé. If none of these is available, I will settle for those rather ordinary Hershey Kisses.

I suspect that this addiction may be genetic because I have a twin sister on the West Coast who is in the same fix. Neither of us, however, wants to do anything about it because eating chocolate is such fun.

George Lang
(Owner of the restaurants Cafe des Artistes and Gundel; author, *Nobody Knows the Truffles I've Seen*.)

Three of my favorite words are: *forcemeat*, *dormouse*, and *earthenware*.

Once I even wrote a recipe to include the above words. Stuffed Dormouse.

The animal is stuffed with a *forcemeat* of pork and small pieces of *dormouse* meat trimmings, all pounded with pepper, nuts and broth. Put the dormouse thus stuffed in an *earthenware* casserole, roast it in the oven or boil it in the stockpot. Enjoy!

Also, as you can read in *Nobody Knows the Truffles I've Seen*, I wrote about the Hungarian expatriates roundtable, which usually met at the Oak Room of the Plaza. Ferenc Molnar was a member of a roundtable of Hungarian expatriates and playing self-invented games was a serious part of the group's activities. One day, someone would be talking about the first words he learned in English, then each of us tried to come up with an amusing line, breezily bypassing the truth. None of us, however,

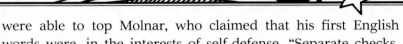

were able to top Molnar, who claimed that his first English words were, in the interests of self-defense, "Separate checks, please."

It turned out to be the favorite words of each of us.

Lewis Lapham

(Essayist; author; editor, *Lapham's Quarterly*)

When I was younger, I wrote a good deal of poetry, most of it in poor imitation of W. H. Auden or Ezra Pound, and I still delight in words for no reason other than their sound. Again for no reason that I can explain, it is the shorter and simpler words that seem to me to hold their place in the dance to the music of time. As follows:

rain
summer
mirth
pear
ruffian
sea
blush
spaniel
rose
Avalon
bawd
crown
dust

Ring Lardner, Jr.
(Novelist, screenwriter, *M*A*S*H*; *The Cincinnati Kid*)

I have always been intrigued by the vast store of obscure words and redundant synonyms in our language, and even in my present state of "caducity" (frailty of old age), I relish some of them for their sound: "glabrous" (smooth, devoid of hair); "susurrus" (gentle murmur, whispering, rustling); "gallimaufry" (jumble, hodgepodge). Others I value because, while not in common use, they have meanings that are relevant and applicable to the world we know: "ergophobia" (fear or hatred of work); "iatrogenic" (caused by a physician, as of a medical disorder); "misology" (hatred or distrust of reason, reasoning, or discussion). I believe much of American public opinion is the result of misology.

Robin Leach
(Host, *Lifestyles of the Rich and Famous*)

Alliterations such as "extraordinary excitement," "majestic monied moguls," "born beautiful," etc. I use alliterations both on television and in ordinary conversations because I appreciate words and the way they can dazzle and delight!

David Leavitt
(Author, *The Lost Language of Cranes*)

My own favorite word is *madrugar,* a Spanish verb which has no equivalent in English. It derives from *la madrugada,* in Spanish the period between late evening and early morning—roughly, 2 to 6 A.M. To *madrugar* is to go out and behave wildly during the *madrugada.*

Richard Lederer

(Author, Anguished English; The Gift of Age; A Tribute to Teachers; and many other best-selling books)

Has there ever been another word as human as "usher?" In sound and meaning it is not a paragon among words, but it contains the full spectrum of humankind. Words and people have always hung around together, and within the brief compass of the five letters in "usher," we find the four pronouns "us," she," "he," and "her." Like humanity, "usher" has a long history, going all the way back to the Latin *ostium,* "doof," related to *os,* "mouth." So there again is that iron link between things and human beings. "Usher" winkingly reminds us that all words are created by people and that language inevitably reflects the fearful asymmetry of our kind. Even though writers write, bakers bake, hunters hunt, preachers preach, and teachers teach, grocers don't groce, butchers don't butch, carpenters don't carpent, milliners don't millin, haberdashers don't haberdash—and ushers don't ush.

Richard LeFrak

(Real estate developer, entrepreneur, CEO of The LeFrak Organization)

My favorite words are "No Vacancy!"

Elmore Leonard

(Award-winning novelist and screenwriter, Get Shorty; Mr. Majestyk; Three-Ten to Yuma)

My favorite words: "cellar door."

Yiyun Li

(MacArthur Fellow; author, Vagrants; Gold Boy, Emerald Girl)

I think my favorite word is one I use in *Gold Boy, Emerald Girl,* "kindness." It is what counters the dark and bleak in life ... kindness.

Art Linkletter
(Radio and TV host, producer)

Some favorite words:

> murmur
> lullaby
> dawn
> consolation
> butterfly

Gordon Lish
(Editor, teacher, author)

Just between you, me, and the lamppost, I guess I probably could be pretty successfully accused of a certain felonious partiality for "that," for "which," and for "whereas." Not (gee, "not" "not"—hey, isn't that a honey for you right there, not to mention, hard by, the old voluptuary "a" itself?) that I ever would dare ever to ever fess to such an avidity—ever! ever!—in a place that is this (actually, give me a "this" over a "that" any day of the week, you know?) public. Look, so far as my shooting my mouth off for the record goes, suppose we just say this—that I am willing to be dead set against any word that looks as if it might want to give even preliminary evidence of its wanting to keep on squatting around making an issue of its sovereignty, all smugly preoccupied out of all proportion with its not ever being susceptible to its ever being genial to the idea of its ever goddamn succumbing to anyone's ever wanting to deform it, which is why, for your information, the more vacant the word—the blanker, the more detachable—the more likely I am likely to be prepared to go ahead and give it a tumble, given that less of anything laden with otherness can maybe keep on getting away with its still being so viciously and so maliciously and so antilishiously stuck to it. Ah, but who's kidding who? Words? Count on it—there is not one blessed one of them that, given half a chance, wouldn't come rushing in and commit homicide—or just as bad, get you killed for it.

Phillip Lopate

(Essayist, author, *Writing New York*; *Notes on Sontag*; *The Phillip Lopate Reader*)

"Austere" has been a favorite word of mine since my movie-mad adolescence, when it rhymed, sort of, with "auteur." It conjures up the cold Danish hush of Carl Dreyer films, puritan pastors moving through white-walled rooms in black garb; a formalist necessity, inevitability, severity in art that thrilled me when I came to understand it. I doted on the sternness of Piero della Francesca, Dürer, Mondrian, Bach, Bresson, Webern. As it turned out, I did not become a particularly austere writer, but one who treats words as intrinsically impure, multipliable, to be used unceremoniously and not worshiped. But I still shudder a little when I see the onomatopoeic "austere." The first syllable raises its hand like a traffic cop, stops us in awe, freezes us like the glint of gold (*au*). The second trembles un-Englishly between the sound of "steer" (castration-fear), "stir," and "stare." I like that; awe-stare, stare in awe at this simple, grave construction. A consecrated space. The Rothko Chapel.

Yet "austere" also carries in its wake the shadow of Astaire, that most graceful, seemingly unRothko-ish performer. Still, beyond Fred's technical perfection, is not what we cherish about him his austere devotion? That severe, bony face and thinning hair, so far from the handsome, sulky luxuriance of Gable and other male stars, and when he danced, he wasn't sexy, or even trying to be, like Kelly, but economical, hieratic, addressed to a concentrated mysterious perfection of the line, trimming away all Rubenesque fat or blur.

"Austere" conveys the ascetic pleasures of sublimation and restraint. I have also been partial in my time to "rigorous," "intransigent," and "recalcitrant." All these circle around the concept of Limit. Others chafe at limit; I relax into it. When I do not set limits for myself, I find them all too easily within myself. Part of my love of "austere" and a morality of borders can be explained as a reaction to my chaotic childhood. My operatic mother monopolized emotion, giving it a hysterical

cast (but then, "hysteria" and "austere" are not so far apart in sound, suggesting a buried, doppelgänger relationship). My father, on the other hand, was somber, grave, and infuriatingly withdrawn. It has been my yearning to cultivate a third path, a calm interiority and outward gregariousness, in which emotion still burns, albeit with an austere, controlled flame.

"Austere" also brings to mind "wisteria." Such is my limited knowledge of the plant kingdom that I am unable to summon any image of that species, though its name has a plaintively wistful suggestiveness, and one can never have too much wistfulness.

Shirley Lord
(Author, *The Crasher*; beauty director, *Vogue*)

I know my husband has been far more "punctilious" about responding to your fascinating letter, which is embarrassing as I am very fond of the word and realize in my books that words beginning with the letter *p* appeal to me—"powwow," "pulchritude," and—yes—"punctuate," too. Beats me as to why, but there it is.

Iris Love
(Archeologist; discoverer of Temple of Aphrodite at Knidos)

There are so many special, engaging, descriptive, and just plain fabulous words in the richest language in this world; that it is very difficult to choose one, much less several.

However, pushed to the fire I will give you five; just in case someone else has already chosen mine.

Here they are: atavistic; illustrious; exquisite; revelation; and regeneration.

Robert Ludlum

(Author, *The Icarus Agenda*; *The Osterman Weekend*;
The Bourne Identity)

"Dissembler"—Such a soft-sounding word that connotes such evil—which, I suspect, was why it was one of Shakespeare's favorites in the area of villainy.

"Savant"—Certainly not in everyday usage, but it conveys a person of overwhelming yet mysterious access to knowledge. Fascinating!

"Resplendent"—Roget's gives it three classifications: "bright," "gorgeous," "illustrious." I think it's all three and then some. For me it also speaks of posture, dignity, even morality in the best sense, if you like.

Roa Lynn

(Author, *Farewell Rio*)

I like a word that embodies its meaning within its sound, dances and somersaults within its sound. "Shimmer" is an example. Other wonderful words: cringe, tinkle, grimace, farrago, thump, squirt, mumble, wisp. The sound unlocks an imagined scene, the sound puts me in the action, tells me what to be suspicious of and what to believe in. It's not just onomatopoeia—maybe you need to know English to know what these words mean, but they could all be acted out by amateurs and the speaker of Portuguese or Turkish would understand. They are "sound glimpses," perhaps into a room that has no fourth wall.

Yo-Yo Ma
(Grammy Award-winning cellist)

After much deliberation in my office as to what my favorite words are, I have come to two choices. The first, "genuine"; the second, "incredible."

I use the word "genuine" a lot because it marks a subject or an object of integrity and sincerity, which are qualities I consider to be absolutely necessary in whatever one does.

I find that an unconditional love of life, and a continual quest for knowledge and new ideas, are what keep me motivated. For this reason I often find myself using superlatives. I find that life is "wonderful," "terrific," "unbelievable," and particularly, "incredible."

I genuinely hope that this is what you are looking for, and that your book turns out to be an incredible success.

Sirio Maccioni
(Owner, Le Cirque restaurant, New York)

"LIFE." Sirio Maccioni's favorite word!

Jamie Malanowski
(Author, *Mr. Stupid Goes to Washington*; *The Coup*)

My favorite word is "yes." It is a word of intimacy, enthusiasm, agreement, permission, encouragement, excitement, vision, triumph. "No" is a necessary word, wise to the world's vicissitudes, Most of the world's troubles come from a failure to say "no" at the right time, but most of my regrets come from not having the courage to say "yes" more often.

Yann Martel
(Mann-Booker Prize-winning author, *Life of Pi*;
Beatrice and Virgil)

My favorite word is "Up." I especially like it with a capital *U* when it resembles a cup with its little curlicues.

Peter Mayle
(Author, *A Year In Provence*; *A Dog's Life*)

My fondness for particular words stems from two sources. Either the delightful associations that they conjure up—lunch, claret, and royalties, for example—or the enjoyment that I find in words of a special pungency. My English teacher at school once reduced me to a mystified silence by calling me a prolix youth, and I have treasured prolix ever since, as well as its close cousin, logorrhea. After living in France for several years, I have developed a penchant for *merde* and its derivatives, but nothing can beat the way a Frenchman pronounces himself disgusted with something. "*Deguelasse,*" he will say, and you feel that he almost needs to take a bath afterwards, such is the horrified relish with which he says it.

Patrick McCabe
(Author, *Butcher Boy*; *The Dead School*)

I have decided that my favorite word is "gawk," or "gawky," which my *Roget's Thesaurus* files along with "clumsy," "awkward," "uneasy," and "gauche." But to me, as I trawl the smoky summer days of my childhood, "gawk" is more than that—it immediately conjures up images of hapless rustic fellows who would relentlessly, unyieldingly, breathlessly pursue you in the course of your day as a seven-year-old, robbing orchards, fishing and trading Batman cards, calling after you as expansive strings of watery mucus threatened to trip them up. "Hi! Hi! Wait for us!" they would yelp, to which the only response could

be: "Where do you think you're going, gawky?" or "Here he comes again—the gawk!"

All this is not to suggest that my affection for the word is solely due to its powerful, bazooka-like onomatopoeia, its pejorative cruise missile-like directness. *Mais non*. It also somehow manages to evoke a certain sympathy for the lambasted unfortunates of those fence-climbing, trout-tickling days. It evokes something in you that you figured had long since been lost—an understanding and compassion for all the misfortunate outsiders of this world. Those non-Prince Hamlets, destined forever never to get their legs across the fence, never to belong to "our gang" or any of the gangs of this world. It is this part of me that wants to cry out to them: "Okay, gawks! Come on then! But just this once!" knowing full sure they will be with me forever, calling me "buddy" and "our pal." Yes, that is it without a doubt, *gawk*. Rest assured, Lewis, if you include it, your illustrious lexicon will be gawked at in every bookshop window from here to Honolulu. And, long after everyone else has passed by, they will still be there, excitedly pointing and going: "Look! Look!" unashamed, unreconstructed, gawks defiant until the end of time.

Colum McCann

(Author, *Songdogs*; *Fishing the Sloe Black River*; *Let the Great World Spin*)

I think that in a strange way the word "tomato" is very important to me. It's not a word I love and it's certainly not my favourite—most of my favourite words tend to be unprintable.

I was born in Ireland and have lived there for most of my life. But I've spent a good part of the last decade in the United States, and the idea of saying "tom-ay-to" as opposed to "tom-ah-to" terrifies me. In a strange way I think it would mean a certain loss of my Irishness, a psychological step further away from my country, a sort of movement into international bastardisation. Saying "tomato" as I've always said it somehow links me to my past. When ordering sandwiches at a deli or restaurant, my pronunciation of the word always elicits certain chuckles, but I think I will cling to my version of "tomato"—along with other words—for as long as I can. So, if I someday say "toma-ay-to." I hope to be able to—as the old song goes—"call the whole thing off."

P.S. I hope you will be able to use this even though it's not exactly my favourite word. Unfortunately, my favourite word—"bollocks"—is perhaps unprintable and it doesn't exactly lend itself to easy explanation!

Pamela McCorduck
(Author, *The Edge of Chaos*; *Machines Who Think*;
The Futures of Women: Scenarios for the 21st Century)

"Frog." What a friendly, endearing word for a friendly, endearing creature. It's nice in German too: *Frosch*. It appears as a nickname in our household in both languages, though usually with the diminutive: *Froggie. Froschlein*. (The cover of the Manhattan Yellow Pages claims "Frog Dealers" as a category of listings, but look inside and you're disappointed: from "Freight Forwarding" to "Frozen Foods" in one hop.) "Fluid" is another word that seeps into my conversation and writing with unusual frequency. "Frugal." *F*-words. They could begin a friendly kiss.

I'm drawn to other words too: "glamour," for instance. That seems a very 1930s word, evoking platinum blondes and top hats, silver fox furs and Art Deco. The love affair was sealed when I read its etymology, deriving from *gramarye*—enchantment, magic—and brought to modern attention by Bobby Burns: "Ye gipsy gang that deal in glamour/And you deep-read in hell's black grammar/Warlocks and witches ..."; its roots to be found in the Indo-European *gerbh*—scratch or carve—and so related to a host of writing words: "epigraph," "autograph," "graffiti," and "grammar."

I'm partial to "snuggle." To "architectonic." To "celestial." To "mantissa," a mathematical term I don't quite understand, so can't drop it casually in conversation. Still, if I were an aristocrat, I'd like to be the Countess of Mantissa.

Patrick McGrath
(Author, *Trauma*; *Asylum*; *Spider*)

As an inky-fingered English schoolboy with a great deal more interest in the frog in my pocket than the contents of a Hillard and Botting grammar, Latin *or* Greek, I was skeptical about the benefits of a classical education. What on earth (I muttered) could be the point of studying *dead languages?* Conjugations and declensions, pluperfect tenses, subjunctives, gerundives, and infinitives—I'd have dumped the lot in a minute.

Wiser counsels prevailed. When I closed a Hillard and Botting for the last time, huge, stodgy lumps of those despised dead languages had been thoroughly stuffed into my head, never to be forgotten or dislodged. There they lay, festering in some neglected mental cellar, until, at an advanced age, and in a state of near-desperation, I turned to fiction as my last best hope of earning a living.

Then at last I got it. Words, beautiful words—the more classical in origin, the better I liked them. "Omnivorous." "Magnanimous." "Concupiscent." "Pantechnion." Large words that broke down into smaller words, yielding their meaning in the process. "Callipygian"—having beautiful buttocks! "Microcephalic"—having an abnormally small head! "Hydrostatics"—the science of fluids at rest! What joy, to bring forth these glorious mouthfuls, though what, for me, was truly exciting was the slowly dawning realization that one could *make them up oneself.*

"Umbrelliferous"—holding an umbrella, as in "She experienced considerable stiffness in her umbrelliferous arm."

"Phlegmosaurian"—concerning a dinosaur whose bones were dug up slightly charred, as in "A passionate argument erupted over the Phlegmosaurian thighbone."

"Bibulophiliac"—one who likes a drink, as in "No Bibulophiliacs."

We owe it to the English language to give it a word or two during the few brief, fleeting moments we're privileged to use it. What better resource than the dead languages that are its soil, its compost? And this, finally, I suggest, is the real point of studying the classics. They facilitate "necrolinguistic neologizing."

Ed McMahon
(TV personality, *The Tonight Show*; *Star Search*)

I find your project very interesting. For years I have been a big W. C. Fields fan and have done a poor imitation of him. He was fond of words that could be used to exemplify his style of speaking. I have picked that up. For example, Fields would say something like: "How fortuitous"; "The lovely digits of your beautiful hand have captured my heart. Allow me to participate."

He was always using words to propel his comedy. I find I'm using words that have to do with success. Words like: "endeavor," "persevere," and "continuity." Words that have something to do with getting there, striving successfully, reaching your goals. Anything to do with words like that pleases me.

Larry McMurtry
(Pulitzer Prize-winning author, *Lonesome Dove*; Academy award-winning screenwriter, *Terms of Endearment*; *The Last Picture Show*; *Brokeback Mountain*)

Well for me I like words having to do with plains, because I'm writing a plains narrative. In fact, the whole tetralogy is a plains narrative set on the plains. I've just finished this immense first draft of *Commanche Moon*, and I haven't looked back at it yet, but I have a feeling that when I go through it, if there are one or two words that predominate, they'll be prairie, plains, grass, something like that.

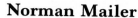

Norman Mailer

(Two-time Pulitzer prize-winning author; The Executioner's Song; The Armies of the Night; Harlot's Ghost; On God: An Uncommon Conversation; The Castle in the Forest)

"Resonance," "dread," and" presence" are, I fear, the words I call upon all too often.

Elaine Marks

(Author, Marrano as Metaphor; Colette; Simone de Beavoir; Germaine Brée professor of French and Women's Studies, University of Wisconsin, Madison; Modern Language Association)

After receiving your letter, I immediately began to have a rush of words. Here are some of them and some comments about them:

Precious, luxurious, tedious, voluptuous, gorgeous, fabulous, fractious, serendipitous, posthumous, joyous, polymorphous, ubiquitous. Of course, I noticed immediately that they all end in *ous,* and that this suffix, which is the ending of many adjectives, means: "full of: abounding in: having: possessing the qualities of" (*Webster's*).

The very first word that came to mind was "portmanteau" as in "a portmanteau word." Again, it is an adjective, proposing a blend, or a "combining of more than one use or quality" (*Webster's*). Undoubtedly, the French connection plays a role in my pleasure, but also, like the adjectives that end in *ous,* beyond what delights the ear and the eye, beyond the signifier, the signified proposes richness, abundance, fullness. It is precisely that richness, abundance, and fullness that words, representing as they do a central absence, make present.

Peter Martins
(Tony Award–winning ballet master in chief,
New York City Ballet; choreographer)

My favorite word is "stunning" because it applies so appropriately to my world.

Bobbie Ann Mason
(Author, *An Atomic Romance*; *Nancy Culpepper*)

My favorite word: "gigglesome."

Familiar words like "lonesome," "handsome," and "adventuresome" are from a whole family of words that include some surprises that have fallen into disuse. I heard Red Barber one morning on the radio say the air was "chillsome." Others are "grievesome," "toilsome," and "boresome." My favorites of these old words are "gigglesome" and "playsome," both usually applied to high-spirited children.

Daphne Merkin
(Literary critic, essayist, and novelist,
The New York Times Magazine; *Tablet Magazine*)

Subfusc … under the radar. I first read the term in P. N. Furbank's eloquent biography of E. M. Forster and have applied it since then to everything I can find that might possibly fit it. Including my life.

Dina Merrill
(Actress, *Desk Set*; *Butterfield 8*; *Operation Petticoat*; *The Courtship of Eddie's Father*)

My favorite swearword is "rats." I don't like to use four-letter words (except this one!) in polite company or in front of my kids, so "rats" works well for me. I seem to remember my father using it the same way when I was kid.

Ricardo Montalban
(Actor, *Fantasy Island*; *Star Trek: The Wrath of Khan*)

My favorite word, for obvious reasons, is "love."
Phonetically, I like "consuetudinary."
Descriptively, I like "adumbrate."

Lorrie Moore
(Author, *A Gate At the Stairs*; *Birds of America*;
Who Will Run the Frog Hospital?)

Favorite words that I'm drawn to? That I think are beautiful? *Summer evening* ... or just *evening. Summer* could be problematic.

David Morrell
(Author, *First Blood*; *The Fifth Profession*;
creator of the character Rambo)

My favorite words are those with which every story I tell begins in my mind. I never fail to experience a rush of emotion as they occur to me. Optimistic and uniquely human, they express our capacity for wonder, our ability to create. I'll be walking down a street or sitting at my kitchen table, watching a movie or reading a newspaper, and the words suddenly come unbidden to me. "What if?" a voice inside me announces. "Suppose A did B. Suppose this happened to C. Suppose D didn't know about E and ... Yes. What if?" Through the alchemy of those two words, something new comes into the world.

Desmond Morris
(Zoologist, author, *The Naked Ape*)

"Xoloitzcuintli"—the Mexican hairless dog. A small domestic dog specially bred by the pre-Columbian Indians for use as a bed heater or "hot-water bottle" to keep them warm at night. Its lack of hair gave it a skin of high temperature.

The word is a favorite of mine for the simple reason that I can pronounce it correctly (Shol-low-its-quint-lee).

"Remarkable" is a wonderful word to use when faced with something that you do not like, but which politeness prevents you from criticizing. When Winston Churchill was shown a portrait of himself by the modern artist Graham Sutherland, he described it, in his acceptance speech, as "a remarkable example of modern art." He later had it secretly burned.

"Neophilia," meaning "the love of the new." I introduced this word in the 1960s to contrast with the already commonly used "neophobia," meaning "fear of the new." Being unusually neophilic myself, I am delighted to see that it has now found its way into the latest edition of the *Oxford English Dictionary*.

Frederic Morton
(Author, *The Rothschilds*; *Thunder at Twilight*)

My favorite word is "cleave." It means "to adhere to firmly and closely." It also means "to divide by a cutting blow." (Definitions from the current *Webster's Collegiate Dictionary*.) The word haunts me because it reflects the paradox to which we life-hungry mortals are born.

Georgette Mosbacher
(Author; CEO, Borghese; political fundraiser)

My two favorite words are *Oh my*. They say so much. As a child, profanities were taboo. Reared to be a lady in all circumstances, my mother and grandmother forbade swearing. But sometimes a swearword says it all. Sometimes a good four-letter word works. So *Oh my* became my phrase, my outlet. I said it loudly, relishing the power of the words. To vent anger, release frustration, moan disappointment, and vocalize shock. I said simply, *Oh my*.

Now I see the splendid, full spectrum of these two small words. As my own experience of life deepens, the colors of meaning inherent in this simple phrase grow richer and more

sublime. *Oh my* fills the air when a good four-letter word is called for and, because they're still listening, it keeps me out of trouble with my mother and grandmother.

Walter Mosley
(Best-selling author; *Devil in a Blue Dress*; *The Last Days of Ptolemy Grey*; *When the Thrill Is Gone*)

Torque, tug, infantilism, capitalism, and yellowy.

Jerome T. Murphy
(Professor and dean, Harvard University Graduate School of Education)

"Zest" is a favorite word of mine. I treasure people who keenly enjoy living, those vital souls with a zest for life. Like a lemon peel in a drink, they conquer dullness and add zip.

Susan Nagel
(Author, *Mistress of the Elgin Marbles*)

Favorite word:

Pamplemousse, which means "grapefruit" in French, because when you say "*pamplemousse*," your lips form a kiss and it tickles!

Audrey Niffenegger
(Author, *The Time Traveler's Wife*; *Her Fearful Symmetry*)

I have a lot of verbal tics like "brilliant" and "you know," but favorites, let me see ... A friend of mine just got married at the Oxford Oratorio, the Church of Saint Aloysius, and I've been going around saying, "Aloysius, Aloysius."

Sigrid Nunez
(Author, *A Feather on the Breath of God*; *Salvation City*)

Some of my favorite words are the names of flowers: hyacinth, jonquil, hollyhock, delphinium, columbine, dandelion, larkspur, rose. It seems most flowers have beautiful names. Foxglove, lavender, libelia, gentian, dahlia, camellia, trillium, wisteria, chrysanthemum. There are some wonderful exceptions: toothwort, beardtongue, toadflax, vetch. I don't know the difference between buttercups and creamcups, inkberries and bunchberries, smartweeds and sneezeweeds, rue anemones and meadow rues, but I adore their names. I am pleased to know that somewhere out there grows something called pipsissewas.

Joyce Carol Oates
(Pulitzer Prize-winning novelist, poet,
Black Water; *Them*; *Zombie*)

"Phantasmagoria. "Chiaroscuro." "Palimpsest." "Intransigent." Why are these among my favorite words? I think because of their sounds as well as their meanings; and their hidden meanings, for me as a writer, as well as their explicit, dictionary meanings. They suggest depths and dimensions of mystery.

Sidney Offit
(Television personality, editor; curator, George Polk Journalism Awards; president, Authors Guild Foundation; novelist, *Memoir of a Bookie's Son*; *The Adventures of Homer Fink*)

I fell in love with the word "chimera" when I was fifteen years old and the managing editor of the student newspaper of the Valley Forge Military Academy. I was desperately in need of a vocabulary to distinguish my editorials from the hut-two-three-four compositions of senior cadets. "Chimera" was everything I thought a word should be—and more. It had classical derivations: "she goat" from the Greek and "a fire-breathing monster with

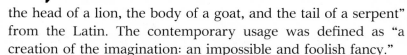

the head of a lion, the body of a goat, and the tail of a serpent" from the Latin. The contemporary usage was defined as "a creation of the imagination: an impossible and foolish fancy."

I never said the word because I was unsure of how to pronounce it; but I exploited the ace of my vocabulary in print frequently, recklessly. I anointed Chamberlain's "peace in our time," the Maginot line, and character-building sessions of the academy's commandant as chimeras. By the winter of 1948 I expressed my frustration with the Henry Wallace presidential campaign in the editorial pages of the campus newspaper of the Johns Hopkins University by dubbing the Progressive Party candidate a "chimera."

Later, my favorite word provided the inspiration for a novel for young readers, *The Adventures of Homer Fink.* It is the story of a Baltimore schoolboy who believes in Greek deities. For several decades *Homer* appeared in various editions and sold briskly. I was beginning to believe I had achieved the writer's dream: a minor classic. Several years ago *Homer* went out of print. My illusions of literary immortality were "a foolish fancy"—a chimera.

Ben Okri
(Booker Prize-winning author, *The Famished Road*;
Songs of Enchantment)

My favorite word of the moment is "illumination."

Frank Oz
(One of the creators of the Muppets;
voice of Bert, Grover, and others)

I don't have a favorite word (however, if I did, "Frumkes" would be right there at the top of the list—if you allow names to be words). One word does strike me as most interesting, though. It is "onomatopoeia." I think I like it because it sounds so much like what it is.

Cynthia Ozick
(Author, *The Shawl*; *Foreign Bodies*; *Dictation: Quartet*; *The Din in the Head*)

"Pellucid," because of both the (limpid, lucent) sound and the nearly utopian slant of meaning. An intensity of clarity—of light, of openness, of truth, of person, of history. "Pellucid" suggests—or promises—that nothing more than the thinnest, most transparent membrane lies between longing and enlightenment.

Abraham Pais
(Physicist, friend and biographer of Albert Einstein)

The choice is hard. But one of my life's mottoes is:
  "The situation is impossible, but not hopeless."

Orhan Pamuk
(Nobel Prize-winning author, *Snow*; *The Museum of Innocence*)

My favorite word is "Dream." In fact, my daughter's name means dream in Turkish.

Richard Panek
(Author, *Seeing and Believing*; *The 4% Universe*)

I don't know about favorite words, but I love starting sentences with "but" or "and"... words you're not supposed to start sentences with.

Linus Pauling
(Scientist, Nobel prizes in chemistry and peace)

I feel strongly about the expression "peace and friendship," for obvious reasons.

There are also a number of words used by physicists and chemists that appeal to me, but would not appeal to the public in general. I shall accordingly say that my favorite word is "parallelepiped." It is pronounced parallel-epi-ped. *Epi* means "around" and *ped* means "faces." A rectangular parallelepiped has six faces perpendicular to each other, each face being a rectangle. Many people write the word as "parallelopiped," and pronounce it parallel-o-pi-ped. This spelling and pronunciation are wrong.

I remember that about sixty years ago I used the word "parallelepiped" in my lecture, and one of my brightest students jumped suddenly, indicating to me that he was astonished. I think that he decided that finally he had caught me making a mistake.

Arno Penzias
(Nobel laureate in physics)

My favorite word is "affidavit."

The first English word I ever learned—Germany, 1938. As a Jewish child in Nazi Germany, I heard the grown-ups talking about this evidently wonderful thing they all wanted. Fortunately, my family got one at the last minute and we were able to come to America.

Regina Peruggi
(President, Kingsborough Community College)

Picking out favorite words is like asking me to pick out favorite students—I love them all and each one for a different reason. But here are three words that I like, all for very different reasons.

The first word is "unconscionable." Though I rarely use it

when I write, I love to say it, for its sound seems to resonate its meaning. So, when I'm absolutely aghast, shocked, or overwhelmed with the injustice of it all, "unconscionable" always seems the most fitting way to express my sentiments.

The second word I've chosen is as soft in sound to me as the first is harsh. That word is "cherish." I like it better than almost any other term of endearment, for the word "cherish" epitomizes for me the feeling of keeping something or someone at the very deepest spot of my heart.

Finally, growing up in the Bronx, I had certain words that I would call part of our very own vocabulary. We drank "egg creams," played "potsy," went to the movies at the Lo-wees (Loews) Paradise and knew that "irregardless" of what other people said about us, people from the Bronx were the best. Somehow, "irregardless" of my schooling, I've never let it interfere with my education in the Bronx!

Steven Pinker
(Johnstone Family Professor of Psychology at Harvard; author, *The Stuff of Thought*)

I like the irregular verbs of English, all 180 of them, because of what they tell us about the history of the language and the human minds that have perpetuated it.

The irregulars are defiantly quirky. Thousands of verbs monotonously take the *-ed* suffix for their past tense forms, but *ring* mutates to *rang,* not *ringed; catch* becomes *caught; hit* doesn't do anything; and *go* is replaced by an entirely different word, *went* (a usurping of the old past tense of *to wend;* which itself once followed the pattern we see in *send-sent* and *bend-bent*). No wonder irregular verbs are banned in "rationally designed" languages like Esperanto and Orwell's Newspeak—and why recently a woman in search of a nonconformist soul mate wrote a personal ad that began, "Are you an irregular verb?"

Since irregulars are unpredictable, people can't derive them on the fly as they talk, but have to memorize them

beforehand one by one, just like simple unconjugated words, which are also unpredictable. (The word *duck* does not look like a duck, walk like a duck, or quack like a duck.) Indeed, the irregulars are all good, basic English words: Anglo-Saxon monosyllables. (The seeming exceptions are just monosyllables disguised by a prefix: *became* is *be- + came*; *understood* is *under- +stood*; *forgot* is *for +got*).

There are tantalizing patterns among the irregulars: *ring-rang, sing-sang, spring-sprang, drink-drank, shrink-shrank, sink-sank, stink-stank, blow-blew, grow-grew, know-knew, throw-threw, draw-drew, fly-flew, slay-slew; swear-swore, wear-wore, bear-bore, tear-tore.* But they still resist being captured by a rule. Next to *sing-sang* we find not *cling-clang* but *cling-clung*, not *think-thank* but *think-thought*, not *blink-blank* but *blink-blinked*. In between *blow-blew* and *grow-grew* sits *glow-glowed. Wear-wore* may inspire *swear-swore,* but *tear-tore* does not inspire *stare-store.* This chaos is a legacy of the Indo-Europeans, the remarkable prehistoric tribe whose language took over most of Europe and southwestern Asia. Their language formed tenses using rules that regularly replaced one vowel with another. But as pronunciation habits changed in their descendant tribes, the rules became opaque to children and eventually died; the irregular past tense forms are their fossils. So every time we use an irregular verb, we are continuing a game of Broken Telephone that has gone on for more than five thousand years.

I especially like the way that irregular verbs graciously relinquish their past tense forms In special circumstances, giving rise to a set of quirks that have puzzled language mavens for decades but which follow an elegant principle that every speaker of the language—every jock, every four-year-old— tacitly knows. In baseball, one says that a slugger has *flied out*; no mere mortal has ever "flown out" to center field. When the designated goon on a hockey team is sent to the penalty box for nearly decapitating the opposing team's finesse player, he has *high-sticked,* not *high-stuck.* Ross Perot has *grandstanded,* but he has never *grandstood,* and the Serbs have *ringed* Sarajevo with artillery, but have never *rung* it. What these suddenly regular verbs have in common is that they are based on nouns: to hit a fly that gets caught, to clobber with a high stick, to play to the grandstand, to form a ring around. These are verbs with noun roots, and a noun cannot have an irregular past tense connected to it because a noun cannot have a past tense at all—what would it mean for a hockey stick to have a past tense? So the irregular form is sealed off and the regular "add *-ed*" rule fills the vacuum. One of the wonderful features about this law is that it belies the accusations of self-appointed guardians of the language that modern speakers are slowly eroding the noun-verb distinction by cavalierly turning nouns into verbs *(to parent, to input, to impact,* and so on). Verbing nouns makes the language more sophisticated, not less so: people use different kinds of past tense forms for plain old verbs and verbs based on nouns, so they must be keeping track of the difference between the two.

Do irregular verbs have a future? At first glance, the prospects do not seem good. Old English had more than twice as many irregular *verbs* as we do today. As some of the verbs became less common, like *cleave-clove, abide-abode,* and *geld-gelt,* children failed to memorize their irregular forms and applied the *-ed* rule instead (just as today children are apt to say *winded* and *speaked*). The irregular forms were doomed for these children's children and for all subsequent generations (though some of the dead irregulars have left souvenirs among the English adjectives, like *cloven, cleft, shod, gilt,* and *pent*).

Not only is the irregular class losing members by emigration, it is not gaining new ones by immigration. When new verbs enter English via onomatopoeia *(to ding, to ping),* borrowings from other languages *(deride* and *succumb* from Latin), and conversions from nouns *(fly out),* the regular rule has first dibs on them. The language ends up with *dinged, pinged, derided, succumbed,* and *flied out,* not *dang, pang, derode, succame,* or *flew out.*

But many of the irregulars can sleep securely, for they have two things on their side. One is their sheer frequency in the language. The ten commonest verbs in English (*be, have, do, say, make, go, take, come, see,* and *get*) are all irregular, and about 70 percent of the time we use a verb, it is an irregular verb. And children have a wondrous capacity for memorizing words; they pick up a new one every two hours, accumulating 60,000 by high school. Eighty irregulars are common enough that children use them before they learn to read, and I predict they will stay in the language indefinitely.

And there is one small opportunity for growth. Irregulars have to be memorized, but human memory distills out any pattern it can find in the memorized items. People occasionally apply a pattern to a new verb in an attempt to be cool, funny, or distinctive. Dizzy Dean *slood* into second base; a Boston eatery once sold T-shirts that read "I got schrod at Legal Seafood," and many people occasionally report that they *snoze, squoze, shat,* or *have tooken* something. Could such forms ever catch on and become standard? Perhaps. A century ago, some creative speaker must have been impressed by the pattern in *stick-stuck* and *strike-struck,* and that is how our youngest irregular, *snuck,* sneaked in.

George Plimpton

(Author, *Paper Lion; Mad Ducks and Bears; Edie: American Girl;* editor in chief, *The Paris Review*)

"Wimbledon" is my favorite word, especially when the tournament is held there and I imagine myself getting at least to the semifinals.

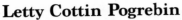

Letty Cottin Pogrebin
(Feminist, founding editor, *Ms.* magazine;
author, *Among Friends*)

My favorite word is "onomatopoeia," which defines the use of words whose sound communicates or suggests their meanings. "Babble," "hiss," "tickle," and "buzz" are examples of onomatopoeic usage.

The word "onomatopoeia" charms me because of its pleasing sound and symbolic precision. I love its lilting alternation of consonant and vowel, its tongue-twisting syllabic complexity, its playfulness. Those who do not know its meaning might guess it to be the name of a creeping ivy, or a bacterial infection, or maybe a small village in Sicily. But those acquainted with the word understand that it, too, in some quirky way, embodies its meaning.

"Onomatopoeia" is a writer's word and a reader's nightmare but the language would be poorer without it.

Roman Polanski
(Academy and Golden Globe Award–winning director,
Chinatown; *Rosemary's Baby*; *The Pianist*; *Tess*)

One of my favorite words is *kurwa*! A dirty Polish word meaning "whore." A favorite swearword of my compatriots.

Reynolds Price
(Author, *Blue Calhoun*; *Kate Vaiden*)

I know that my favorite words in childhood were two—"Reynolds Price." By the time I was five or six, I'd get off alone and repeat them tonelessly until they became a kind of protective spell. Was I preparing myself for a lifetime of pernicious narcissism, or was I just unearthing the normal born-writer's obsession with words for their own sake? I vote for the latter.

Since then I've been aware of certain words that tend to recur in my writing, but I can't say that their use gives me

unusual shivers of pleasure. Take a single example—the word "dense." I'm always having to weed its excess appearances out of manuscripts and proofs; and aside from the fact that I may just be a congenitally dense human being, I can't honestly guess why the word insists on volunteering in my work.

Come to think of it, though, it's a worthy syllable—dense itself in sound and brevity and as elegant in its homely pressed-down compactness as I've always wanted my speech and life to be.

W. V. Quine
(Author, American philosopher; former Edgar Pierce Professor of Philosophy Emeritus, mathematics, Harvard University)

I am pleased and flattered by your invitation to celebrate my favorite words. I hate some words, mostly latter-day coinages that gratuitously mix Latin and Greek. On the other hand, I am at a loss for favorites. Donald Davidson once told me that I overdo "actually," but I have been unaware of any particular fondness for it. If I have reacted by using it more than ever, it has been in a spirit rather of self-mockery or bravado.

Nahid Rachlin
(Author, *Veils*; *Married to a Stranger*; *Foreigner*; *Persian Girls*)

"Sky" is my favorite word. Every time I look at the sky it is changing—in color, brightness, shape. In its flowing change I can imagine possibilities, hope ...

Dan Rather
(Emmy and Peabody-Award winning anchor, *Dan Rather Reports*)

My two favorite words carry strong associations with my parents. When you think about it, they were the first people to teach me the use of language, so I guess it stands to reason that my favorite words remind me of them.

My father's word was "courage," a word that meant a lot to him beyond the dictionary meaning: coming from his mouth it was a one-word pep talk in tough times. A fine old word—"take heart"—and a benediction I continue to invoke (but no longer on the *CBS Evening News*). My father tried all his life to give his children the things we'd need, not just dinner on the table but tools for the future. Courage—the word *and* the spirit—he gave us aplenty. On my best days, I hope I'm worthy of my father's legacy, at least a little.

In the neighborhood where I grew up, there was a field or vacant lot that my mother always called a "meadow." It was the most beautiful word she knew. Mother was strong and gentle, and "meadow" has a strong and gentle sound: the stretch of the short *e* and the long *o* clipped off. For my mother, the word conjured images of sunshine and peace, of nature that didn't threaten even if it wasn't altogether tamed. Those images fit my mother, too.

James Redfield
(Author, *The Celestine Prophecy*; *The Tenth Insight*)

My favorite words are "trust synchronicity," which has to do with mysterious coincidences.

Lynn Redgrave
(Actress, *Gods and Monsters*; *Georgy Girl*)

"Jibber." Used in our household as a word to describe any kind of remote control device (TV-video-garage door-gate opener). We don't know how we came to use this word—but strangely, not only our children but also stray visitors and acquaintances seem to know exactly what we are talking about. Even my eighty-three-year-old mother in England now knows what a "'jibber'" is. "Jibber," what a satisfying word!

Leni Riefenstahl

(German filmmaker/photographer, *Triumph of the Will*;
Olympia)

My favorite word is "passion" because "passion" is the root of
all creative work.

Joan Rivers

(Comedienne, actress)

I like "cellar door." It's the most beautiful-sounding word in
the English language. If you say it as one word, it *is soooooo*
pretty.

P.S. My second favorite word is "money," and my third and
fourth together are "rich person."

Graham Robb

(Author, *The Discovery of France*; *Parisians*)

I suppose my favorite word is "boulangerie." It's a word and a
place that I come back to again and again. For me it's Paris ...
I can stand in a boulangerie and drink in the tastes and smells
of the city.

Ned Rorem

(Pulitzer-prize-winning composer, author,
Nantucket Diaries; *Knowing When To Stop*)

As vowels suggest colors to the poet Rimbaud, and as chord
progressions suggest crystal-orange birdsong to the composer
Messiaen, so words, all words, are for me no less strong for their
dictionary meaning as for their associative textures, mainly *of*
food and various cloth material.

Thus "one" implies dried blood, "three" is melted butter,
"five" is old cherry pie, "twenty" is the taste of a dime. And thus
my favorite word is the omnipresent and humbly useful "the".

"The", for me, is the hue and feel of tan-gray goose feathers on a cool summer night.

A. M. Rosenthal
(Pulitzer Prize-winning columnist and former editor,
The New York Times)

PRESIDENT to SECRETARY OF STATE: "Who thought up this Bosnia plan?"
SECRETARY: "I did, sir."
PRESIDENT: "Well, I've seen some ridiculous plans, but you can bet your sweet patootie this one is really cockamamie."

Jack Rosenthal
(Pulitzer Prize-winning editor in chief,
The New York Times Magazine)

Let me cast my lot with the word "palmetto." It became a metaphoric favorite about ten years ago when my son John came home from high school with a vocabulary list whose words he declared to be "stupid and useless." What with SATs drawing near, I inspected the list and pronounced the stupid and useless words to be inspiring. "Well, no one ever actually uses those words," John insisted. "You would never use them in *The Times*."

You know what happened next. I took the list of words and, during the course of the next week, worked all twenty into one or another editorial. Words like "alabaster" and "antiquity" were easy; the hardest, as you've already divined, was "palmetto," but I finally got that in, too.

Only to be immediately deflated. At home that night, John had a new list. "These are even dumber words," he said. So I worked all twenty new words into editorials the following week. And then, the week after that, came parents' visiting day. I couldn't resist rushing up to Susan Sherman, the English teacher, to describe my exertions in support of her vocabulary

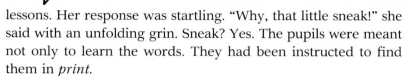

lessons. Her response was startling. "Why, that little sneak!" she said with an unfolding grin. Sneak? Yes. The pupils were meant not only to learn the words. They had been instructed to find them in *print*.

So when you ask for my favorite word, I have five hundred to choose from, since I ended up getting the whole term's list onto the editorial page—"timorous" and "truculent," "cantata" and "cantilever," "attenuate" and "reverberate." But one word stands tall; "palmetto," gracefully fanning the air and marking the maturing of a son who had his father's number.

Henry Rosovsky

(Lewis P. and Linda L. Geyser University professor of Economics; former Dean of Arts and Sciences, Harvard University; principal architect of the core curriculum)

I am enclosing a copy of my favorite words and they are the quote from Master William Johnson Cory of Eaton as cited in my book *The University: An Owner's Manual.*

> You are not engaged so much in acquiring knowledge as in making mental efforts under criticism. A certain amount of knowledge you can indeed with average faculties acquire so as to retain; nor need you regret the hours that you have spent on much that is forgotten, for the shadow of lost knowledge at least protects you from many illusions.
>
> But you go to a great school, not for knowledge so much as for arts and habits; for the habit of attention, for the art of expression, for the art of assuming at a moment's notice a new intellectual posture, for the art of entering quickly into another person's thoughts, for the habit of submitting to censure and refutation, for the art of indicating assent or dissent in graduated terms, for the habit of regarding

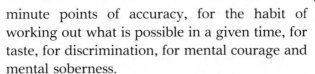

minute points of accuracy, for the habit of working out what is possible in a given time, for taste, for discrimination, for mental courage and mental soberness.

Above all, you go to a great school for self-knowledge.

I love these words because they are the best description of a liberal education that I have ever found.

Wilbur Ross
(Banker, CEO, W. L. Ross & Co. LLC)

"More" was the theme song of that great movie *Mondo Cane* and of my first wedding. The marriage failed so I dropped the song but found another use for the word. Now, in every corporate restructuring, I say over and over and over, "more, more, more" until the proponents of "less" give up.

After years of living with "more," I began to understand how important it is to everything we do. "More" is the issue between management and labor, landlord and tenant, parent and child, husband and wife, politician and taxpayer, addict and pusher. Americans who say "More" more than one hundred times per day are much more likely to become richer and have better sex lives than those who do not. "More" also was the Yuppie buzzword.

Despite the word's significance, the etymology of "more" is unclear. Some reputable scholars trace it to the pagan god of plenty, Erom, which a dyslectic translator made into "more." Equally unreliable sources ascribe the root of "more" to the archaic Latin "moreleisa," which was the approximate weight an average slave could carry one mile up a 10 percent grade. When slavery ended, the newly liberated Italian workers absconded with the "lessa," whom they worship to this day, leaving more for management. My personal favorite theory is that the word emanated from the Plattdeutsch *Muchen moren moster*; a superlative originally applied to outstanding lager

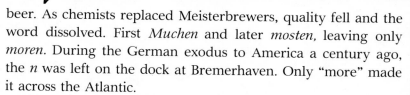

beer. As chemists replaced Meisterbrewers, quality fell and the word dissolved. First *Muchen* and later *mosten,* leaving only *moren*. During the German exodus to America a century ago, the *n* was left on the dock at Bremerhaven. Only "more" made it across the Atlantic.

Wherever it came from, "more" is better, so go for it. I have.

Howard Rubenstein
(Attorney, CEO, Rubenstein Associates Inc.)

My list of favorite words includes:

"Monster"—Denoting an enormous achievement that is felt throughout the City of New York.

"Mediate and negotiate"—In a city that is as diverse as New York, these two actions are among the most important efforts business, community, and government leaders can participate in.

"Pride"—This word is defined as being a New Yorker. We take pride in being the nosiest, the most creative, the brashest, and yes, even the rudest if that's what it takes to get the job done.

"Schlep"—Yiddish in origin. Anyone who works on Seventh Avenue uses this word with the ease of their native tongue to describe what they have been doing all day.

"Excel"—The standard of competition in a very demanding environment. As you linger on the word, you can almost hear the tires screech away from the competition.

"Ethical"—The moral compass by which to steer professional and personal behavior.

"So?"—For all intents and purposes, a greeting but reflective of the Jewish tradition of asking "why" even when there isn't a question on the table.

"Novel"—In a world that bores easily, creating something novel and creative still generates respect.

"Great!"—This word remains one of the simplest yet most effective exclamations in our vocabulary. You rarely see anyone exclaim, "Mediocre!" It is "great" that commands respect.

William Ruddick
(Philosopher, ethicist)

For some years I have found "prolepsis" indispensable in philosophical discussion of a number of issues, especially in medical ethics. We often *leap ahead* in regarding and treating beings and events more developed or mature than they are. We tend to talk and act as if things are already what we expect them to become. If optimists, our prolepses prematurely describe our chickens as if hatched. For example, we describe fetuses, or even embryos, as babies or children. If pessimists, we interpret disturbing events as if they not only were omens of disaster but were disaster itself. Thus, the clinical signs of irreversible coma become the criteria of brain death which is taken to be death itself. Prolepsis is a feature of teleological thought, the tendency to describe and understand things in terms of their mature states or intended outcomes. As such, prolepses give us more confidence in the forming of expectations and projects in an unpredictable world than would descriptions focused more narrowly on present states and events. The English phrases I can think of seem too critical (e.g., "premature anticipation") or inappropriately deliberative ("predictive description"). But admittedly, I have not tried hard to find an English equivalent: the Latin makes the notion both impressive and memorable for my students. (In so doing, I may be regarding them in the converse mode of retrolepsis regarding and treating things as if less mature—a habit of thought that paternalists cultivate.)

Oliver Sacks

(Physician, neurologist, author, *Anthropologist on Mars*;
The Man Who Mistook His Wife for a Hat;
The Island of the Colorblind.)

Dear Lewis,

One of my favorite words is *apocope*—I use it (for example) in "A Surgeon's Life": "... the end of the word omitted by a tactful apocope" (*Anthropologist on Mars*, Vintage, p. 94).

I love its sound, its explosiveness (as do some of my Tourettic friends—for when it becomes a four syllable verbal tic, which can be impaired or imploded into a tenth of a second), and the fact that it compresses four vowels and four syllables into a mere seven letters.

I also like *syzygy* for some of the same reasons and because it has three distinct meanings.

P.S. I also like *zaroe* and *ube*.

Edward Said

(Literary critic, author, *The World, the Text, & the Critic*;
Orientalism; *Culture & Imperialism*)

There are a group of words beginning with the letter *v* that hold a particular pleasure for me. This is only partially connected with their meaning. Words like "virtuoso" and "virtuosity," "voluptuous," "volatile," "vivacity," "vortex," "vertiginous" (or "vertigo," which I find less interesting) and "victorious" (more so than "victory," which seems curiously abstract and a bit disdainful). All these *v* words communicate something exceptional and quite out of the ordinary, a sensation of the extra, the brilliant, even the dangerous, and lots of, well, "vitality." I have realized that I use them in my own writing as a kind of special reward for what I'm trying to say, words not pronounced lightly or immediately but bestowed on an experience or person at the end and after trying in many other words to put my finger on something quite unique. Looking recently at a videotape of Glenn Gould playing an extract on the

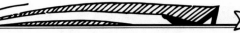

piano from Strauss's *Elektra*—reducing the mammoth orchestral score to a brilliantly complex keyboard version, conducting it with a free hand here, singing the parts of Elektra and her sister Chrysothemis in German there, his face transfigured by the rich complexity of what was going on, his incredibly agile and expressive fingers flawlessly negotiating the music with such inevitability and mastery—and the word "virtuosity" was pulled out of me as if from my unconscious.

My own language, Arabic, doesn't have a *v*, so that there's an additional pleasure in the rare novelty of these words, quite unique to English.

Sebastiao Salgado
(Photographer, *Workers: The Archaeology of the Industrial Age*)

My favorite word is *travessia,* a Portuguese word meaning "our movement." We came from one place and we go to another. We are in travessia in movement, in transition, in passing.

Harrison Salisbury
(Pulitzer Prize-winning journalist,
The 900 Days: The Siege of Leningrad)

My favorite word is "pumpkin." I don't know why. But "pumpkin" touches off some childhood habits of mine. You can't take it seriously. But you can't ignore it either. It takes a hold of your head and that's it. You are a pumpkin. Or you are not. I am.

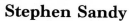

Stephen Sandy

(Poet, *Man in the Open Air: Thanksgiving over the Water*)

"Qualmish." Having a feeling of fear, misgiving, or depression. Excellent word when asked how one feels on Monday morning (i.e., line to use as alternative for the preemptive *kvetch*—instead of "don't ask"). Also has the ring and effect of an indigenous tribe that lived on cranberries, oysters, and quail. "Oh, yes, the Qualmish, they used to banquet on the shores of this river. The middens of their shells are not infrequent among the rushes."

"Scatheless." A hard Scandinavian opening—with an aural effect like "scald" or "scrape" or "scull"—but with a lovely finish, a mellow diminuendo with the voiced *th* and the lingering *l* and dying *s*'s; the first syllable like a spike of vodka; the second, a swallow of venerable Richebourg. And of course it describes that most enviable of conditions: the *unharmed*—nay, more; the word denotes rather the state of being not-get-at-able; not of merely escaping harm, but of *being* off the hook, *being* far from harm's way.

"Pergola." I love this word for its evocation of a time of seeming grace, of sunlit leisure on spacious American afternoons. When I used the word in a class some years ago, a student (he was from the big city) had never heard of a pergola, and asked what one was; the denotative meaning was simple enough, yet he could not get why the word had such an aura for me, so to suggest its connotations, I wrote a poem to explain one word:

> The macadam is flaking and the lilac
> Too big to bloom
> Fingers a cobweb of smoky light from the terrace,
> Grazes the sun-chalked cedarshakes. And no surprise.
>
> Gone the lady to Athens or Anjou. Her sunroom
> Oozes silence. The paisley over the back
> Of a wicker rocker. The pedals of her grand hover
> Above the calm sea of the tiled floor.

Like gilt clouds, each brazen ball
Without a claw. In Roseville jardinieres
Iron geraniums stiffen and chip;
A noose of rose and the scum of ferrous

Oxide throttle the sundial's Horatian tip
For those noddy panamas and white-ducks of class.
In the pergola woodflies on the pedestal
Walk all over it. What are years?

Or at the stoned gazing globe's crashed glass
Peek in on themselves, magnified; what's more,
Behold no Chloe or her golfing lover
In the mullioned saucers of their eyes.

Francesco Scavullo
(Fashion photographer)
My favorite word: "Shittheworldisfullofit."
    That's one word.

Mary Schmidt-Campbell
(Dean, Tisch School of the Arts, New York University)
My word is "ineluctable."

Robert Schuller
(Television evangelist, Crystal Cathedral Ministries)
My two favorite words: "Wow!" and "Hallelujah!"

Glenn Seaborg
(Nobel Prize in chemistry, 1951; former chairman,
Atomic Energy Commission)

I have had a number of favorite words that I used especially when our six children were growing up. One of these was "kumquat"; I recall saying "kumquat may" (come what may) and that I wanted for dinner "kumquats and fried rainwater." One of my favorite alliterations was to "derogate, denigrate, deprecate, deride, and decry"; my kids, in later years, claim I was trying to increase their vocabulary, and perhaps they were right. When they were small, I used to threaten, when they were naughty, that I would "impy-do" them or even "roog" them (pronounced like "root" with a hard *g*); I guess I liked the sound of these contrived words. I often say that I am doing something with "impunity"; my wife, Helen, avers that I am referring to a lady friend with the name Impunity. My administrative assistant claims I favor the words "perspicacious" and "perspicuous," and I do admit to liking their sound. Another favorite word is "alacrity" (let's move with alacrity).

Wilfrid Sheed
(Grammy Award–winning novelist, essayist, critic,
The Morning After; *Max Jamison*)

I'm too much of a whore, or philandering philologist, or whatever, to have a favorite word. As soon as I take a shine to one, I realize I've probably been using it too much and it has to go back to the end of the line. So my favorite word is always the one I haven't used lately but which fills the bill perfectly. In the last year or so, I believe I got off a pretty good "plangent" (I wouldn't touch "lambent" with a ten-foot pole) and adequate "ragamuffin," and for the late William Shawn, my first and last "fussbudget"—though don't hold me to this; it might come in handy again if I ever have to write about Ross Perot or Robert Dole.

But there have been hundreds of favorite words over the years that have nothing to recommend them but aptness: they fit the hole in the puzzle, and you have to love a word that does that, even if it's one you wouldn't look at on another occasion. For instance, the word "aptness"; plain as an old shoe, but it gets you from here to there when the "multitudinous seas incarnadine" aren't running. And you can use it twice, because nobody saw it the first time.

Cybill Shepherd
(Golden Globe-winning actress, *Moonlighting*;
The Last Picture Show)

"Ubiquitous"

Alix Kates Shulman
(Author, *Memoir of an Ex-Prom Queen*; *Drinking the Rain*)

Fish is my favorite word. Why? Because it's a four-letter *f*-word usable in any company? Or because it ends in that comforting shshshshshsh-sound? Maybe because it evokes the beloved island in Maine I described in my recent memoir, *Drinking the Rain*, where I spend long summers of solitude; maybe because my first childhood crush was on a soldier named Fish (brother of an uncle-in-law), who looked gorgeous in his WWII airman's uniform; maybe because you can eat it, smell it, swim with it, snorkel over it, draw it, write it. Fish. Love it.

John Simon
(Theater critic, Bloomberg News)

One of my favorite words is "amusisch." It's a negative German word meaning devoid of any gift of the Muses. Another more positive German word that I like is "museal," which means worthy of being exhibited in a museum.

Jane Smiley

(Pulitzer Prize-winning author, *A Thousand Acres*;
Private Life; *The Man Who Invented the Computer*)

My favorite words are all fairly obvious—"garlicky," which is exactly how I like everything I eat. Here's a good recipe:

Peel 16 doves of garlic and rub a little salt and paprika on the pieces of a cut-up 3-pound chicken. Pour a little olive oil into a sauté pan, and toast a 5-inch-long slice of French bread until it is golden on both sides. Take out the bread, and put in the garlic and chicken. Brown them together over medium heat for 15 minutes, then take out the garlic and pour off the fat. Add 1/2 cup white wine and 1/2 cup water. Cook the chicken for 10 more minutes, or until cooked through. Put the garlic, the bread (cut into chunks), the juices from the pot, 1 tablespoon cognac, and 1/2 teaspoon saffron threads into a food processor and process. Add salt and pepper to taste, then reheat the sauce with the chicken. Serve with mashed potatoes. I like Yukon Golds or Rose Golds.

This is a Spanish recipe from *Bon Appétit*. I have never met a recipe for chicken with garlic that I didn't like.

I like the word "baby," because the *b*'s remind me of round baby cheeks.

I like the sound of the words "Krakatoa" and "glistening." Probably the word I tend to overuse most often is "clearly," which I also like very much.

Alexander McCall Smith

(Author of the Isabel Dalhousie Series, and
The #1 Ladies Detective Agency Series)

My favorite word is a Scot's word, "fantoosh," sometimes spelled "fantouche." It means very smart and glittery and special, like a new tie ... Oh! That's fantoosh!

Robin Smith
(CEO, Publishers Clearing House)

A favorite word of mine is "callipygian" (actually I now find I was erroneously using the word, saying "callipygious" instead). Anyway, I like it because it is unusual—and I'm amazed and amused that someone went to the trouble to make up a word for "having shapely buttocks." Another one I like is "cacophony" because it really conveys its meaning—maybe I also like hard syllables.

Albert Solnit
(Sterling Professor Emeritus, Child Study Center, Yale University)

I am not aware of having a favorite word, but as I've been thinking about it, I have a favorite saying that I did not create but which I learned from a distinguished professor of pediatrics, Daniel Darrow, who died several years ago. He used to say (and I have used this over and over again), "When there's too much teaching, there's not enough learning." I have spent a good deal of my life as a teacher who learned some years ago that it is the privilege of the teacher to enable students to become active in learning about what interests them and about what they need to know to help themselves to acquire the competence they seek and the satisfaction they'll gain from being in charge of themselves.

Nicholas Sparks

(Author, *The Notebook*; *Message in a Bottle*; *Safe Haven*)

I think most authors will admit that they love words, and I'm no exception. Words are more than simply the definition provided in the dictionary; frequently they serve to shape the mood and emotive quality of sentences or paragraphs. Some words—for example, "wind-chimes," "whispers," "murmuring," "shadows"—are not only descriptive, but they sound lovely to the ear, and if used appropriately, they enhance the experience of the reader.

Gloria Steinem

(Feminist, author, editor, *Ms.* magazine)

My favorite word is "empathy."

Robert J. Sternberg

(Provost and Senior Vice President, Oklahoma State University; former IBM professor of Psychology and Education, Yale University)

My very favorite word is *Alejandra*. That's the name of my wife, and she is incomparable. One couldn't have a better wife.

After that my favorite words are *schlemiel* and *schlimazel*. The schlemiel, as we know, is the one who spills the chicken soup on the schlimazel. The reason I like these words so much is that they capture so much of what life is about. Some people are constantly dumping on others—that is, there are schlemiels constantly dumping on schlimazels. And the words capture most of abnormal psychology as well. There are those who cause problems for others, and those who allow others to cause problems for them. We have a garden variety of fancy names for them, but we don't really understand why these people are the way they are, and it pretty much boils down to schlemiels and schlimazels again. I have a lot more to say, but people are constantly phoning me and knocking on my door and otherwise

bringing me problems, and I have to attend to them, not to mention wiping the chicken soup off me.

Fred Mustard Stewart
(Author, *Mephisto Waltz*; *Century*; *Ellis Island*; *Six Weeks*)

My favorite word is "chthonic" (pronounced "thonic"), which means "pertaining to the gods and spirits of the underworld." It is my favorite word because I've never seen it used except once, in a *very* obscure English short story. No one has the foggiest notion what it means, and whoever saw a word start with *chth?* I'll admit it has been somewhat difficult to work it into a conversation.

Catharine R. Stimpson
(Dean, Graduate School of Arts and Science at New York University)

"Tomboy!" Say the word, shout the word, chant the word with a crowd.

"Tomboy!" It is a trochee, so stress that first syllable. It is a drumbeat. Next, stretch out that second syllable, that "boy." Make it "buoy." The deep meaning of "tomboy" will reveal itself. Being a tomboy is a declaration of independence that buoys a girl up, sends her up up in the air.

Such is my gnostic reading of "tomboy," my esoteric knowledge revealed through contemplation and experience.

In contrast, the conventional reading of tomboy is condescending, dismissive, or anxious.

According to the *Oxford English Dictionary*, in the 16th century the tomboy was a boy, but a bad boy, a rude and boisterous boy. Then that dangerous creature, the upstart woman, began to behave like the bad boy. She was bold and audacious—romping, frolicsome, leaping, shouting, so uncouth. This hoyden might be a barrel of laughs, but straight men and women also had to watch her hands and lips when she was

around other women. The line of descent from Renaissance tomboy to the modern butch, the dyke, is as clear as a tumbler of light beer.

How was a culture devoted to the binary roles of masculine and feminine to handle this flyaway boundary-breaker? This girl who wanted to act like a boy? This irritant who might prefer top hat to snood? In opera, on the stage, she could put on trousers, the more brocaded the better. She could be a Cherubino, whose delightful voice and winsome ways made masculinity manqué a diversion.

Or, in novels, she could be a tomboy while young, but she would put away laddish ways when she was through with that stage, that phase, we now label adolescence. Tedious Scout, the daughter of saintly Atticus in *To Kill A Mocking Bird*, likes to cuss and use her fists. To her petticoats imprison. But that was then. Now she is the mature narrator of America's favorite novel.

In contrast, the women who cherish and act out the secret history of tomboys never fully grow up. They continue to rebel and romp. They are the zing and zest of freedom, the rattle of iconoclasm. They say tart and shocking things. They ride motorcycles and bicycles and fire trucks. They are fun.

These women are not Petra Pans, however. They hold jobs and pay taxes and raise children. Still, while doing all this, they refuse to abandon or repress the tomboy. She ferments within, yeast in the bread of life.

The tomboys who last beyond adolescence gaze sympathetically at other women who have clamped down on their tomboy past. For they have permanently wounded a source of vitality. Think of Jo March, in *Little Women*. She is in the Tomboy Hall of Fame—next to Amelia Earhart and Katherine Hepburn. But Jo marries that older professor, and runs a school, and now revels, not in her own antics, but in those of her mildly tomboyish boy students.

Dear Jo, poor Jo.

For those of us loyal to our tomboy past, we say the word as if it were the first word of an anthem. Keep on trocheeing, keep on trucking.

Leo Stone
(Psychoanalyst)

A word that has always fascinated me is "irredentist" or "irredentism." It means "unredeemed" and comes from "Italia Irredenta," which was an organization that became prominent in the late nineteenth century for advocating the incorporation of certain neighboring regions into Italy. I use "irredentist" in a more personal way to explain people who are trying to recapture or redeem something in their lives.

Mark Strand
(Pulitzer Prize-winning poet, essayist, *Blizzard of One*; professor of English, Columbia University)

Abacaxi-which is Portuguese for "pineapple."

Morbido—which is Italian for "soft."

"Icebox."

Whitley Strieber
(Author, *Communion*; *The Hunger*; *Wolfen*)

I have hundreds of favorite words. Funny words like "groak" and "uloid" are delicious to say. Complicated ones, such as "hepaticocholangiocholecystenterostomy," captivate me. I love learning to pronounce them with sufficient facility to include them in ordinary discourse. Words of power draw me. And there are such words, such as "unseen," which have great power. The unseen. He is among the unseen. Unseen, she slipped the phial from her bodice. The only explanation left was this: the unseen. And then there are puns and plays on words, usually considered altogether unseemly, but fun all the same.

Elizabeth Strong-Cuevas
(Artist, sculptor)

"AWE," a word we are about to lose, that has been robbed of its meaning by the unfortunate adjective "awesome." "AWE" meaning ecstatic, reverential feeling before Beauty, before the Magnificent. "Awesome," a tiresome word, flung indiscriminately in all directions, on all occasions until it has become so trivial, it is valueless.

"AWE," to be used on rare occasions before the marvelous, the extraordinary. It conveys wonder and amazement. Even the sound conveys a feeling. Saying the word, the mouth opens in speechless delight before that which is greater than the self.

Miguel Syjuco
(Man Asian Literary Prize grand prize-winning author, *Illustrado*)

Nettlesome, *ignominious*, and *equipoise*, because they are beautiful and not used enough.

Gay Talese
(Author, journalist, essayist, *The Silent Season of a Hero*; *A Writer's Life*; *Frank Sinatra Has a Cold*)

"Effulgent." Picked it up as a high school kid reading F. Scott Fitzgerald.

Maria Tallchief
(Prima ballerina)

My mother was a lady of great "courage" and "perseverance." My father had a wonderful sense of "humor" (as did my grandmother Tallchief).

I also like the words "grace" and "elegance."

Amy Tan

(Author, *The Joy Luck Club*; *The Kitchen God's Wife*)

Here's my contribution to your book: *Ing-gai* (ing-gi), auxiliary verb, Mandarin Chinese. (1) should have; (2) when coupled with English, used to express a condition of maternal regret: *Ing-gai* never come to United States to raise children who fight against me all the time; (3) must; ought; when coupled with English, used to indicate a filial form of duty: *Ing-gai* visit Mom this weekend or else we're in big trouble; (4) "*ing-gai* shopping"—the neurotic habit of continuing to look at real estate or the latest computer equipment with the express purpose of torturing yourself with the fact that you spent way too much on last year's purchase.

Etymology. In-gai has been used extensively in Mandarin for thousands of years, but its first appearance in English usage can be traced to a living room in Oakland, California in 1958, when a Chinese mother was heard to say to her six-year-old American-born daughter, "Turn off TV; *in-gai* practice piano." It was popularized by a small group of San Franciscans in 1983 when the same mother was heard to order chicken in a restaurant while everyone else had ordered fish. When the chicken arrived, the mother eyed it suspiciously, looked enviously at the fish on other people's plates, then sighed and remarked, "Tst! *Ing-gai* order fish." Since then, the expression "*ing-gai* order fish" has become a useful way to express small regrets over hasty decisions.

Usage. Today *ing-gai* coupled with English continues to be used in all kinds of lamentable situations. Curiously, when used frequently, it has the power to reduce regret to laughter.

Lionel Tiger

(Anthropologist, professor, Rutgers University; originator of the term "male bonding"; author, *The Decline of Males*; *The Pursuit of Pleasure*; *The Imperial Animal*)

Some of my favorite words served as doodles at an academic meeting at the Stanford Law School.

Badminton	Vast	Violin	Happening
Posh	Tiptop	Peanut	Pituitary
Tub	Flounder	Herringbone	Whitewash
Replacement	Harsh	Wringer	Venture
Notice	Pillule	Pendulum	Picturesque
Nomenclature	Knob	Palliative	Pastor
Tremendous	Pernicious	Horseradish	Table
Penumbra	Puerile	Pantaloon	Kerchief
Posh	Happenstance	Effervescent	Endure
Peroration	Wholesome	Punishment	Hillock
Hiss	Pin	Iberia	Siberia
Folderol	Pond	Holbein	Vim 'n'
Hullabaloo	Tally	Handicap	Vigor
Verisimilitude	Portia	Humility	Voracious
Hollywood	Albertina	Hopscotch	
Hey!			

Joseph F. Traub

(Edwin Howard Armstrong professor of Computer Science, Columbia University)

Here's my favorite word: "Information." In 1959, as a new PhD, my intuition told me that *information* was central to solving certain kinds of scientific problems over a broad spectrum of fields. I began what would be a thirty-five-year research focus on the relationship between information, uncertainty, and complexity, which has eventually evolved into a field in its own right, known as *information-based complexity,* a field that is internationally studied, with its own research journal, and with regular international symposia and workshops.

Roughly speaking, the aim of information-based complexity is to tease out the *laws of information,* just as physicists have discovered the laws of matter and energy. (This is distinct from *information theory,* a phrase coined by Claude Shannon. In a conversation I once had with Shannon, he readily agreed that his celebrated work was a mathematical theory of communication, not information.)

We know that in the real world, information is usually partial or incomplete; contaminated by error; and has costs attached. Knowing that, can we deal optimally with uncertainty? I believe we can. Laws about information would lead to economic solutions when information is scarce and very costly. In addition, laws would facilitate effective resolution of situations where we are inundated by staggering amounts of information that must be scanned with the hope of drawing the best inferences.

I have speculated that laws of information might even lead to problems in science that we could say with assurance were unsolvable, questions whose answers were—no matter how clever we are—forever unknowable.

Laurence H. Tribe

(Professor of Constitutional Law, Harvard Law School; author, *The Invisible Constitution*; *American Constitutional Law*)

Favorite word: "whisper."

Alan Trustman

(Screenwriter, author, *The Thomas Crown Affair*; *Bullet*)

"Celador."

Desmond M. Tutu

(Anglican Archbishop of Cape Town, Nobel Peace Prize recipient)

Words that I like are "tremendous" and "wonderful." They roll out so wonderfully.

John Updike

(Two-time Pulitzer Prize-winning author, *Rabbit Is Rich*; *Rabbit at Rest*; *Couples*; *The Witches of Eastwick*)

When I was a young writer in my twenties, I was told that I overused the word "lambent." Recently at the age of sixty, I received word (sic) that the word "conjuration" appeared three times toward the end of a collection of essays, *Odd Jobs*. I am aware in myself of a fondness for "anfractuous" and "phosphorescent," possibly because that is how the world seems to me.

Andrew Vachss

(Author, *Safe House*; *Blue Bell*; *Blossom*)

"Evil" is my favorite word because its very existence is denied by entire professions, including social work. Everybody is sick, and sick is confused with sickening, so when somebody does something utterly abominable, instead of looking in a mirror and saying that's evil, we say, "Well, that's sick," and we can understand it. We're the only species that ever existed in the history of the world that allows predators of our own kind.

Sander Vanocur

(American journalist, television commentator and personality)

After shuttling between Nantucket and Santa Barbara for the past fifteen years, I have concluded that my favorite words are "capital," "trust fund," and "probate."

Gwen Verdon

(Tony, Emmy, and Grammy Award-winning actress, dancer,
Damn Yankees; *Sweet Charity*; *Can-Can*;
New Girl in Town; *Redhead*)

Beloved
Providence
Junie Moon—My Cat
Morning
Farewell

Patricia Volk

(Author, essayist, columnist, *To My Dearest Friends*)

I've always been partial to *fuh-drayt, fuh-shimmeled, fu-cocktuh, fuh-blondjet,* and *fuh-tushted.* I was even thinking of starting a singing group called The Five Fuhs. These words are all different but interchangeable. They mean crazy, mixed up, addled, lost, and wiped out. Just saying them and shrugging makes you feel better. I also love the Italian word for raincoat, *impermeable,* because saying it is like being in an opera. And in high school biology, I fell in love with "euglena." I use "euglena" every chance I get, as in "It's raining today. I wonder if that's good for the euglenas." "Euglena" is the best word. You can't say it without smiling.

Just for the record, my least favorite word is "dearth." I can never remember what it means because it sounds like the opposite.

David Foster Wallace
(Author, *The Broom of the System*; *Infinite Jest*)

That's an interesting question. Sometimes a word will come up over and over again when I'm enthralled with the word. The word *troubled,* meaning emotionally unstable, or unhappy, came up like a hundred times when I wrote *The Broom of the System*, and I wrote that when I was in high school.

Tom Wallace
(Literary agent, T. C. Wallace Ltd., The Wallace Literary Agency)

My favorite words? Can anyone who is at all conscious of words and is at the same time halfway articulate have favorites? I guess mine, if they are really favorites at all, have to do with various stages of my life. Prep school: "shoe." Anything admirable, as in "white shoe." College and graduate school: "etiolated." When it comes from Bill Buckley's carefully pursed lips, it sounds *truly* "euphonious." Publishing: a "popcorn read." A sales manager at a publishing house at which I once worked so characterized any books with legs, a book that ran out of the bookstores (i.e., a book whether fiction or nonfiction, serious or frivolous), which was a "page-turner." Literary agent: Can there be any word with the authority and clarity of "commission?" As in 10 percent or 15 percent. Obviously, this does not refer to military rank, presidential panels, or professional baseball, basketball, and hockey potentates. Finally: the word that has meant the most to me in my many years as a student, reader, editor, and agent is "booklover." Someone who can get the same kick from a 5 x 8, 6 1/8 x 9 1/4 paperback or hardcover volume, sewn or perfect bound, that others get from the Sunday *New York Times,* a bottle of champagne, or an extra-inning baseball game.

Wendy Wasserstein
(Pulitzer and Tony-Award winning playwright, *The Heidi Chronicles*)

"Beguiling" is a favorite word of mine. Better than charming, with a little mischief thrown in. On a directive—girls be guiling. I want to learn.

"Coney Island," because I have no idea why "island" is pronounced "eyeland." Shouldn't that be the Pearle Vision Center and not a spot of land amidst the water? But I suppose it's better than being an "isthmus," which sounds like a decongestant on holiday.

Carol Weston
(Author of *Girltalk*; *The Diary of Melanie Martin*)

Favorite words? In English, how about "catnap," "zigzag," "poppycock," or "summertime?" Or maybe just "thank you?" In French, every mother-in-law is a *belle-mère*. In Spanish, *zarzuela* is an operetta and a fish stew. In Italian, my winning word is *bambini*. And speaking of kids, in all four languages, I like "family," *famille*, *familia*, *famiglia*. Thank you!

Nancy Willard
(Poet, novelist, children's author, *In the Salt Marsh*; *The Left-Handed Story: Writing and the Writer's Life*)

The Pamplemousse Observed

Pamplemousse—a word, I thought, straight out of Edward Lear, and without knowing what it meant, I fell in love with the word during a dictation in a high school French class: *Le pamplemousse atteint la grosseur d'un melon.*

To a friend who has never studied French, I said: What do you think pamplemousse is?

It's a pampered moose that lives in Argentina, he replied.

It's the French word for "grapefruit," I told him.

But I go on thinking about that moose in Argentina and the earnest young couple who have moved to the pampas to study and tame it. Every night they leave it an offering of the food it loves best. Every night they call,

"Pamplemousse! Pamplemousse!"

They do not know with what sound the pamplemousse will answer.

Edward O. Wilson

(American biologist, entomologist, two-time Pulitzer Prize winning author, *The Ants: The Diversity of Life*)

"Abyssal." It implies the deep, the dark, and the unknown of the planet's surface.

Gahan Wilson

(American author, cartoonist, *The New Yorker*; *Playboy*; *Edgar Allan Poe: Masters of the Weird Tale*)

The best and most resounding personal favorite word I ever heard was Edgar Poe's "cellar door," and I certainly hope you feature it prominently in your book.

I never noticed it until you asked me, but I don't really have an *objet d'art* kind of favorite word, the kind you keep in a niche and admire. My favorite words all seem to be functional.

For example: I can always depend on "pumpkin" to cheer me up.

"Ineffable" helps me increase awareness in the presence of something deserving a good deal more than ordinary attention.

"Good" is the real workhorse. It brings nice things closer every time. You can't beat it for inner glows.

Enclosed find the signed contract. "Contract"* is a word I don't much like, come to think of it.)

*As a term of the said contract, let the party of the first part (the above-mentioned Frumkes) understand that the words of Wilson (henceforward to be referred to as "the contributor") must be labeled "functional" and their purpose clearly given, or the contributor's choices will make no sense soever. Oyez, oyez.

Frank Wilczeck

(Nobel Prize-winning physicist; Herman Feshbach Professor of Physics at MIT; author, *The Lightness of Being*)

Defenestration

In Prague you can see it—the actual window. In 1419, an enraged mob stormed town hall and defenestrated the judge, the burgomaster, and thirteen town councilors, setting off the Hussite War. For an encore, in 1618, two imperial governors and their secretary got tossed from the heights of Prague's castle, sparking the catastrophic Thirty Years' War. Not to be outdone, in 1948, communist putschists tossed Jan Masaryk in his pajamas through an upper-story bathroom window at the foreign ministry to his death, also in Prague. Those great events, and several lesser ones, are referred to as the Defenestrations of Prague. They popularized the word "defenestration" (to the extent it has been popularized).

I like the word "defenestration" for several reasons. It makes me think of Prague, which I love. Why? Because for me Prague brings to mind the movie *Amadeus*, which was shot there, and with it pleasant mental echoes of Mozart's music, and recollected images of Tom Hulce's manic portrayal, and especially the deathbed scene, where he dictates his *Requiem* to F. Murray Abrahams' Salieri.

Also, "defenestration"'s five syllables roll off the tongue, and please the ear.

Also, "defenestration" is wonderfully specific, in a way that few words are, apart from proper names.

Also, I've found "defenestration" to be a useful word to bring to mind whenever I'm trapped listening to some tedious blowhard at a meeting. On those occasions I find it diverting, and soothing, to imagine an appropriate defenestration.

It's an interesting challenge to work "defenestration" into conversations that don't happen to be centered on violent political quarrels, showy methods of suicide, or Prague. One way is to casually observe that "'Defenestration' is euphonious," thus efficiently incorporating two beautifully ripe words into one short sentence. I've tried it, with interesting results.

Hilma Wolitzer
(Novelist, *Hearts*; *Summer Reading*)

Favorite Words: "morosely" and "wistful."

One of the first books I read on my own as a child was *Penrod* by Booth Tarkington. It opens: "Penrod sat morosely upon the back fence and gazed with envy at Duke, his wistful dog." I didn't know precisely what "morosely" or "wistful" meant, but I felt the *mood* of that sentence, and I think I fell in love then with the mystery of language.

Stuart Woods
(Edgar Award-winning author, *Chiefs*; *Orchid Blues*; *Imperfect Strangers*; *Dead Eyes*)

One of my favorite words is "tergiversate," which the *Oxford Concise Dictionary* says means, "equivocate, make conflicting or evasive statements." Reason: once, in my youth, I won a writing contest, along with a dozen other folks. The prize was a sumptuous lunch at Voisin, then a famous French restaurant in New York. Weeks passed, however, and the lunch never materialized. Finally, each of the winners wrote a letter to the contest organizer, all mailed on the same day, asking what happened to our lunch? Each of the letters, somewhere in the text, used the word, "tergiversate." We got our lunch.

Paul Zindel
(Pulitzer Prize-winning playwright,
The Effects of Gamma Rays on Man-in-the-Moon Marigolds;
children's book author, *The Pigman*)

My favorite word is "concupiscence."

William Zinsser
(Author, *On Writing Well*; *Writing to Learn*)

I don't have a collection of favorite words like "williwaw" that I keep in a display case to moon over. Such words delight me with their music when I see (and hear) them, but unless they fill a precise need—"filigree," "lapidary," "oscillate"—I shy away from using them, wary of being sucked into the bog of pomposity where academic monsters like "adumbrate" and "ineluctable" lurk. My favorite words, which I spend a lot of time rummaging for, are hundreds of simple, vivid replacements for words that are just too dull to give writing a sense of freshness. "Brazen," for example. Used instead of "bold," not only does it take the reader by surprise with its piquant *z,* but its sound perfectly conveys its meaning. A brazen scheme is more than merely bold; listen and you'll probably hear a mountebank. I write by ear, and sound is usually what leads me to what I'm groping for. I still remember the pleasure of finding exactly the word I needed to catch what had exhilarated me as a young GI riding a train across North Africa during World War II, getting my first exposure to the Arab world. It was the Arab hubbub at the stations.

Elmo R. Zumwalt, Jr.
(Admiral, U.S. Navy [Ret.])

My favorite word is "retromingent."

I thought it was particularly intriguing when Ben Bradlee, then editor of *The Washington Post,* reportedly used it in describing Reed Irvine of Accuracy in Media.

My second most popular word is "supercalifragilistic-expialidocious," which I enjoy using frequently with my grandchildren.